WHEN THERE ARE NO WORDS

FINDING **YOUR** WAY TO COPE WITH LOSS AND GRIEF

by

CHARLIE WALTON

Pathfinder Publishing

Ventura, California

WHEN THERE ARE NO WORDS

Published by:
Pathfinder Publishing of California
458 Dorothy Avenue
Ventura, CA 93003
(805) 642-9278

Library of Congress Cataloging-in-Publication Data

Walton, Charlie, 1940-
  When there are no words : finding your way to cope with loss and grief.
  / by Charlie Walton.
    p. cm.
  Includes bibliographical references and index.
  ISBN 0-934793-57-3
  1. Bereavement —Psychological aspects. 2. Death—Psycho logical aspects. 3. Grief. 4. Walton, Charlie, 1940- . I. Title
  BF575.G7W344 1996
  155.9'37—dc20   95-38853
                                                        CIP

DEDICATION

For Kay

CONTENTS

1

WHEN THERE ARE NO WORDS

Someone who loves you a lot wants desperately to lessen your pain. They are yearning for some magic words... for a few concise, over-the-counter phrases... that can encapsulate all of human wisdom and explain away the pain you are feeling since part of you has been ripped away without benefit of anesthesia.

But... *there are no words.*

As long as there have been humans... and as long as there has been death... the search has continued. People who love you are aching to fix what's broken. They want to kiss it and make it well. They recall their successes at consoling young children who had skinned their knees. They want to do the same for you. Cheer you up... hold you tight... divert your attention to a more pleasant topic.

But the words that fall naturally from their mouths in times of tragedy don't help much. "I am so sorry" is without doubt the leader of our verbal efforts at consolation. The one set of words I remember hearing most often as people stepped forward to try and express the inexpressible was, "Oh, I am so sorry."

They say they are sorry and you mumble your appreciation. But you can tell that... as soon as their words are out... they are disappointed that they didn't say something better. A voice from deep inside them begins immediately punishing them: "What a thing to say! 'I'm sorry' is what you would say if *you* had done something to cause this. You didn't do anything. You are simply filled with sorrow because of the bad thing that has happened. Of course, you are sorry. Who wouldn't be sorry under the circumstances? You should have thought of something more helpful to say!"

"I am so sorry." It's the truth. It's direct. Yet it makes the speaker feel so ineffective. Those who come to console go home feeling like failures... failures as friends... clumsy friends unable to fix what's broken... unable to kiss it and make it better. But the death of a loved one is not a broken tricycle. Some things cannot be fixed.

Someday... when your friends have had their turns at what you are going through now... they will finally understand that it made absolutely no difference *what* they said. Their words do not register in your mind anyway. What is important is that they came... they suffered and they were frustrated alongside you.

You *feel* their presence and you *understand* their messages of love... regardless of the words they offer. In moments of human loss, words often get in the way of the communications that *can* help.

Now... when I go to comfort a friend... having had the experience of being the bereaved one... I know there *are* no words. No words are necessary. Everything that needs to be said is communicated in the presence, the look, the touch, and the shared silence. If I am sorry, they are going to know it. If I am something greater than sorry... something for which our language has no terminology... the message will be clearly communicated.

The only valid thing I know to say is that I don't know what to say... and that goes without saying. In the weeks and months that follow, there will be time for words. But... at the moment of separation... there really are no words.

2

WISH I DIDN'T KNOW NOW
WHAT I DIDN'T KNOW THEN

I wish I weren't writing this book. I wish I didn't think I have something to share with you. I wish I didn't identify with your grief. I wish I could go back to a cold December 15th and erase from history the event that introduced me to the death of loved ones.

Around our house, we still categorize events as happening "before the boys died" or "after the boys died." Like most families, we had experienced the predictable deaths of older family members. The deaths of parents and grandparents are expected. They are bound to come. They are part of the natural sequence of life. Some people live long. Others not so long. When you bury the people in the generation ahead of you, it is with sadness and resignation. But, when you bury your own children, life is suddenly and terribly *out of proper sequence.*

In the first days after the boys died, more than one person told me, "Charlie, you should write about this." They knew that I made my living as a writer and they assumed that the writing would be therapy for me and a service to others struggling under the same sort of burden.

At the time... standing with my nose pressed hard against the trees... I was in no position to pontificate about the forest. I thanked them for the encouragement but declined the invitation. "Maybe later," I said.

It's later.

I'm ready now to try and share a few things with you. I hope they help. They won't make your burden any lighter... but they may help you feel a little less like the only one who has ever been as heartbroken as you feel right now. You might as well know that you're going to have to carry the full weight of this load. There is a sense in which others will do what they can to bear your burden... but you are the only person on the earth who can carry this one.

You're the one who is going to deal with it twenty-four hours a day. When the others have cried themselves to sleep, you'll still be awake. When they are beginning to sigh and shake their heads and return to their lives, you'll still be searching for someone in charge... someone with jurisdiction to reverse what appears to you to be an obvious violation of cosmic justice.

A lot of your coping ability in the first few months is going to stem from habits you've previously developed for dealing with the frustrations of life. The death of your loved one is probably the greatest frustration you will ever encounter. Every cell in your body is going to ache to do something to fix the problem. It cannot be fixed... and grief is the result.

Sometimes, grief comes out in the form of violence. I have listened to grieving parents tell about destroying lamps and chairs and walls because they are so frustrated and angry. If violence helps you and doesn't hurt anybody else, I say go ahead and trash the stuff. You can buy more furniture... perhaps cheaper than you can live with the bottled up anger.

I've never been a smasher. Like most folks I know, I have the equally dangerous habit of turning anger and frustration inward... eating away at stomach linings and heart valves instead of smashing a lamp. I might be more likely to lash out with a razor-edged comment at someone... inflicting even more lasting damage but in a more socially-acceptable way. Make yourself remember however... that those who are going through your grief with you make especially easy targets for anger. But... unlike broken furniture... human trust can never be fully replaced. As you let your anger out, remember their vulnerability.

It's hard not to want to hurt somebody when death has slammed the door on your heart. But... if you can manage it... try to be *nice* while you are going through it. There's no use in compounding your burden by lashing out at those around you. They mean well but are constitutionally prohibited from carrying your load... because they are not you.

You have to carry the whole load. The straps on this pack fit your shoulders only. That's just the way it works. Your closest friend can't do it for you. You're going to live through this one the same way you're going to pass through your own death... all by yourself. And afterward... you'll know that God knew what he was doing when he set it up that way.

Some grieving people I have met have told me that the support of fellow church members made all the difference for them. Unfortunately, an equally large group has angrily recounted abandonment and desertion by its ministers and fellow church members. You can be sure that the grief process is about to show you who your real friends are, what you truly believe, and where your real trust lies.

If the last thing you want to hear right now is "the religion thing," I promise you that the following pages are not going to come at you with a lot of churchy platitudes and syrupy sayings. The shelves are already full of those kinds of books and they did nothing but discourage me. My intention on these pages is to tell you what happened to our family and what we have learned with the passage of time. Our church family *was* a tremendous help to us... but church membership doesn't always make grief any easier.

Of course, "easier" isn't really a valid way of measuring pain. It doesn't reduce anybody's pain to find out that someone else has suffered a more tortuous death or a numerically-greater loss. There is no "easier" or "harder" when it comes to grief. It just hurts... and its limits coincide with yours. However much pain you can stand... that's how much it's going to hurt.

You can count on some well-meaning person reminding you that the Bible promises that you won't be tempted beyond that which you can endure. What they will fail to mention is that the same Bible also gives every indication that an evil one is alive and well and fully dedicated to pushing you to your limit and keeping you there for as long as possible. Jesus never promised his listeners that their faith would protect them from pain... or death... or protracted grief.

You are going to have to carry your burden the full distance. No short cuts. No magic slogans from posters or bumper stickers to suddenly "snap you out of it." The good news is that you are a whole lot stronger than you think you are. You can believe me when I say that... even though I have not met you personally... I share your grief. It is my prayer that... in these first lonely hours of embarking on your journey... it will help you to hear a story from one who's well along the way.

The day will come when a good friend will look back with you at the hell you are going through today. Your friend will shake his or her head and say, "I just don't know how you made it through all that. I just don't think I could do it."

And you will smile and respond, "It's not a thing anybody can make it through... until they have no choice. Once there's no choice... you do it... one painful breath after another."

3

3:25 A.M.

Middle of the night.

The light goes on in our bedroom.

I squint my eyes and look at the digital clock. One-inch tall, fire-red numerals burn the time permanently into the back of my brain. Three. Two. Five.

Kay is standing next to our bedroom door with her hand on the light switch. "Charlie," she says, "There's a policeman here."

What comes out of my mouth is something like, "I'll be right there." What is going through my mind... as I climb out of bed and step into a pair of jeans and a sweater... is a combination of partial thoughts. "Do I really sleep so soundly that Kay can answer the door and I never even know she's gotten out of bed?" The answer, proven many times through our marriage, is a clear yes.

"What have those kids gotten themselves into this time?" I wonder as I walk barefooted down the hall. With three sons... born about two years apart... we have had teenagers around our house for twelve years. Like every parent of teenagers, we do our share of hand-wringing. In the earlier years, we stayed awake every night until all chicks were safely back in the nest and tucked away. Now... with our oldest engaged and living in his own apartment and our youngest half-way through his nineteenth year... we are soon to be out of the teenager business.

Now... when the boys go out at night... our aging eyelids just can't stay up as late as our sons can. The boys are becoming independent. The parents are becoming sleepy. So, Tim and Don... the two still living at home... come and go on their own schedules. Sometimes we find them in their beds in the morning. Sometimes their beds are empty and... later in the morning... they call to explain that they stayed at a friend's instead of driving home late.

Or... it is equally likely that we will check beds in the morning and find an *extra* sleeping teenager. Don's best friend, Bryan, is as likely to be sleeping at our house as at his house during school vacations. The two boys have been the closest of friends since the day they met at age two. They are nineteen years old and share a seventeen-year friendship that has endured the entire spectrum of stages that so often come between young friends.

Now... with Bryan home from college for his Christmas vacation... and Don home on Christmas leave from Honduras where he has been assisting a medical missionary... there is no predicting where the two will be spending the night. The one sure thing is that there will be a lot of laughing and giggling whenever the "Bron Club" is meeting. Does friendship get much closer than having a single name for two people? The first two letters from Bryan's name... the last two letters from Don's name... and the exclusive two-member Bron Club is in its seventeenth year.

Kay and I stop halfway across the den. I put my right arm around her waist and my left hand reaches for the cold wrought iron of the spiral stairs that wind up to the loft where Tim's room is. Though that moment is now many years into the past, I can close my eyes and feel the cold, squared edges of those steel rods that were welded together to form that staircase.

Ten feet away from us stands a white-headed, pot-bellied county policeman. He stares down at the clipboard in his hand. He seems ill at ease.

I am not ill at ease. I have been the parent of teenagers long enough to know that the parade of traffic tickets and broken bones and crumpled fenders goes on and on. I am calmly braced for the next problem in the odyssey of raising children. Whatever bones are broken, we will follow doctor's orders until they heal. Whatever the cost, we will find a way to come up with the money. However embarrassing it is, we will work our way through it.

The policeman looks down at his clipboard. "Do you have a son named Timothy Charles Walton?"

"Yes."

"Do you have a son named Donald Wayne Walton?"

"Yes."

"They are both dead."

We both gasp. Kay sags slightly on my right arm. My left hand makes every effort to bend the steel rod it holds. My mouth and throat are immediately dry and the question that comes first to my mind emerges in a rasping voice. "What happened?"

The policeman does not change his monotone. "We don't know for sure. We think it might be a combination of things. They were found in a black Audi less than a mile from here. There were no signs of foul play. And there was another person with them."

"Who?" I rasp... trying to think who it might have been. Perhaps Linda, Tim's girlfriend. Perhaps Warren, Don's buddy when Bryan is away at college.

The policeman's eyes return to the clipboard and he struggles to pronounce the name.

"Oh, no!" Kay and I breathe together, "Bryan was with them."

From the very first instant of the officer's clumsy announcement of our sons' deaths, my mind processes information calmly... too calmly. I understand. I comprehend. I hate it... but I think through the implications and alternatives. My mind never goes blank. It doesn't even shut down temporarily as I might have expected. I long to lose control... freak out... scream... faint. Those seem like the appropriate responses... the natural human responses that I would write if I were scripting this scene for television. But those responses are not my nature. One of the standing jokes in our family is that "Dad is always calm and controlled in emergencies — it's daily life that makes him fall apart!"

I process immediately the fact that our baby and the comedian who often introduced himself as "the middle child" are both dead. I am never going to see them again... alive in their familiar bodies. To this day, I have not yet processed the fact that Bryan died with them. Bryan... the only son of our close friends... friends we had known since college days... friends with whom we had shared good times and bad.

Kay says, "I think I'm going to be sick." We turn and leave the policeman staring at his clipboard and I help Kay toward the bedroom. Her knees become weaker and weaker and finally give way as we reach the bed. She collapses onto the bed. I lift her feet up.

"Are you going to need the trash basket?" I ask. Kay and I have endured morning sickness together through three pregnancies and I am a practiced hand at grabbing a plastic trash basket, dumping its contents onto the carpet, and getting it quickly to her bedside.

"I think I'm going to be okay," she replies. "Could you get me a cold wash cloth?"

I run cold water over a wash cloth, put it on her forehead, and walk back into the room. The officer is standing in the same spot. I walk past him into the kitchen, open the refrigerator, and pour a large glass of orange juice. I drink it without stopping. My mouth and throat still feel dry. I pour another glass and drink it.

The policeman comes into the kitchen. "I'm sorry to have to give you the news like that... but that's the way they teach us to do it. They say it's better to come right out with it instead of trying to say it gradually."

"It's okay," I say. "Can you tell me anything about the cause of death?"

"No," he says, looking back down at his clipboard. "We won't know for sure until after the lab reports but... like I said... it looks like it was a combination of things... but no evidence of foul play."

"Well, we thank you for coming," I say, feeling a sudden desire to have this man out of our house. I move toward the front door.

"Oh, I'm supposed to stay until somebody gets here for you," he says. "We have a police chaplain I can call if you don't have a preacher of your own."

"That won't be necessary," I say, continuing toward the front door. "We have a very close church family and I will call some of them right away. Thank you for coming."

"But don't you think I ought to wait until somebody gets here for you?"

I open the front door. "It won't be necessary," I say in a monotone. "Thank you for coming."

The policeman and his clipboard go through the door, down the steps, and into the morning darkness. I walk into my office, turn on the light, and sit down at the desk. I dial the phone number for Rob and Karen. They are close friends from church and Rob is scheduled to go with me later in the morning to a business appointment.

The phone rings once and Karen answers. She sounds alert and as frightened as any normal person is when the phone rings in the middle of the night. I am concerned that Rob not have to get up early and dress for a business appointment that I obviously am not going to keep. I tell Karen what has happened.

Her response is calm and measured. "We'll be right there."

I hang up the phone and call Jerry. Our minister and my close personal friend for many years answers his phone as if it is not unusual for it to ring in the middle of the night.

"Jerry, it's Charlie. I'm sorry to call you in the middle of the night but we've got a monumental catastrophe on our hands." I tell Jerry what has happened. I tell him that Rob and Karen are on the way. He says that he will need to make some phone calls and then he will come.

Two more calls: Bob and Carole are Bryan's parents. Bud and Carole are our other close friends from college and church. Three couples with one heart... six kindred souls struggling through the career-building, child-raising years together.

At Bryan's house, Carole answers. A county policeman arrived at their door at the same time the officer arrived at ours. Carole is calm though her voice and mine tremble as we talk. We exchange only a word or two about the terror of the thing that has happened. We go more directly to the subject of what we are going to do next... or more accurately... *where* we will do it. The phone conversation is very much as if Carole and I are arranging a social get-together for our regular three couples.

The decision is that... at least initially... Bob and Carole will come to our house. It is a typically unselfish gesture for Bryan's parents to leave their home and drive the twenty or thirty minutes to our house.

I go back to check on Kay. She is up and getting dressed. I tell her that Rob and Karen are on the way over and that Bob and Carole and Bud and Carole are also coming. I decide to take a shower before everyone arrives. I climb into the shower, turn the water on full blast, stick my face into the hot waterfall, and try as hard as I can to cry.

If you grew up as a male in America, you will have no trouble understanding my frustration at being unable to cry. "Big boys don't cry" was more than *taught* to us — it was ingrained... instilled... injected into our chromosomes. Even though I have lived through three decades that have softened the ridiculous macho myth... even though I have raised my own sons to know that it is okay to cry when you hurt... I still find myself unable to cry because of sad things that happen.

Strangely enough... I cry for *happy*... but not for *sad*. Something beautiful or beautifully done can leave me misty-eyed. If a young child combines its innocence and its limited grasp of the language to beautifully articulate an idea, I have tears running down on my smile. When an idea is perfectly phrased or a difficult task perfectly executed... I have a lump in my throat and blurry vision. When the movie makers combine color and light and musical crescendo to make human emotion larger than life... when the lovers find each other... when *Rocky* wins the championship... I cry for happy. But for real pain, for actual sorrow, for life's true frustrations, I need to cry but the tears won't come.

I mention my difficulty in crying because it is so representative of the most important thing I have learned about grief. As I stood there in the shower struggling to make tears, I was having my first introduction to the most important lesson that was to come out of the whole "monumental catastrophe" that entered our lives that morning. I was doing the worst thing you can do as you grieve. I was trying to do what I thought was expected... to do what I thought others would consider appropriate... to live it the way I would have scripted it for actors in a play.

Time after time in the days that followed, I would meet that principle again. In conversations about grief in the years since, I have confirmed the concept with others' experiences: *your natural response to grief is the right response for you.* The worst thing you can do to yourself and to those around you is to try to express your grief according to someone else's formula... or worse still... by some set of behaviors that you *assume* to be standard.

A telltale phrase when you are living through a "monumental catastrophe"... a phrase that should alert you to danger... is "I suppose everyone will be expecting me to... ." When you hear those words going through your mind, stop everything and remind yourself: "There is no one else like me. My grief is one of a kind. Whatever works for me is the right response for my grief."

I am out of the shower, dressed, and into the kitchen for only a few moments before Rob and Karen come driving up. Until we hear their car in the drive, Kay and I stand in the kitchen, holding each other, saying nothing, trembling slightly from moment to moment, but saying nothing.

Rob and Karen come in. More hugs... more standing and hugging and saying nothing and making little gasps for breath. Eventually, hands will demand something to do. We start to perk coffee. Familiar kitchen movements break the conversational ice and... with a few interruptions to set out coffee mugs and sugar and cream... the four of us lean against kitchen counters and talk.

In less than a minute, we can tell everything we know from the policeman. The rest of the seemingly endless conversation spirals in circles through all of the things we *don't* know. In your own monumental catastrophe, you will find that a world of words can be generated by the incessant exploration of questions for which there are no answers... by the proposing of theories to explain the unexplainable. It is perhaps one of our natural human defense mechanisms... filling the air with talk so none of us has to admit how helpless and alone we feel.

When you have to go through something alone, it's helpful to have close friends around you. Kay and I have... since we first met... been each other's best friend. As our love has grown, our bonds of communication and trust have strengthened. Each of us is absolutely confident that... no matter what happens... it will not come between us. It's a rare relationship in these times. It's not a result of our wisdom or knowledge. It's a result of the fact that both of us want that kind of relationship more than we want anything else. It was true when we first married. It was true when the washing machine broke down. And it was true when our boys died.

Kay and I were surrounded by two concentric circles of friends whose loyalty could not be questioned. Though separated by miles, we remain very close to our blood relations. Kay's father and mother have both passed away but she and I remain close to her two brothers and her sister and their spouses. My parents... who are both alive and well... and my younger brother and his family live 250 miles away in Nashville. We have traveled the road to Nashville through the years keeping the family ties strong. Occasionally... when friends and business associates talk to me about their families... I hear more about bad blood than I hear about family solidarity. In the midst of our family tragedy, we at least know we don't have to "walk on eggshells" to keep some long-standing family feud from breaking out. Our family is a blessing.

The other circle of friends... whose loyalty is beyond question... is composed of our spiritual brothers and sisters from church. Kay and I had moved to Atlanta many years before to be a part of this church. We had sold a house, ended a job, and made the move because of a unique spirit of love we saw in this congregation. It was an environment we wanted for ourselves... an environment where we wanted our boys to grow up.

Bob and Carole arrive. Someone else lets them in the door. Kay and I meet them in the middle of the den. We stand silently and hug each other. Hardly a word is exchanged. What can be said? Words only get in the way. It is one of those moments in time when there is too much communication going on to interrupt it with words. When *your* monumental catastrophe occurs and there *are* no words... just let it be that way.

4

SPEED-UPS AND SLOW-DOWNS

As the morning wears on and our house fills with friends, I begin a period of walking in a slow motion world that is simultaneously as normal as any other day and too distorted to be real. Movies and television have taught me to expect some kind of special effects version of an LSD trip... with piercing, overlapping sounds that are too confusing to understand... and spinning, close-up, fish-eyed visuals that are terrifying and distorted. Once again, reality turns out to be nothing like the movies. What *does* happen is normal sound and normal visuals. People come and go. They look the same as they always look. Their voices are not distorted. They are heart-broken over the loss we have sustained together but the surrealistic, mind-bending movie never runs in my head.

My mind does race ahead of events though and I often find myself wondering why it takes so long for simple things to be accomplished. As people begin their sentences, I am fairly sure I know what it is they are going to say and I have to force myself to wait patiently while they work through all the words necessary to get to the end of the idea.

The first time I ride in a car, I can hardly believe how long it takes to go from our driveway to the stop sign at the corner. Normally, that distance is an unnoticed incidental of starting out to go anywhere. But on the morning of the monumental catastrophe... I sit in the back seat of a friend's car... and it takes forever to get to the corner. The ride to the corner is only the first of many boring segments required to make even the shortest drive. When we stop at a red light, it seems to hold for hours.

It is only later that I will realize the degree to which perceptions are altered. Weeks and months later, I begin to realize that things were not as normal as I believed at the time. Friends... who later tell me things that I said or did during the first few days... help me to see that... while I was amazed at how normal everything felt in the midst of such a life trauma... and while I was marveling that I was able to walk and talk and think as though nothing had happened... none of those impressions was true.

Few of us realize how reflexive are the many habits we have developed for social interaction. We are able to walk and talk, meet and greet, even make basic conversational responses as though we were completely present and accounted for when... in reality... our minds are in another dimension... or in no dimension at all. But since mannerisms, questions, answers, even opinions are more reflexive than they are deliberate... I carried on what I thought were normal conversations about the most traumatic of life events... believing myself to be one hundred percent *in the moment*... while my mind had actually switched everything to automatic pilot... so it could go to the back of the plane to sit and stare thoughtlessly at the clouds.

Everything was in slow motion but my kidneys! Anyone who has traveled with me knows that I never pass up a rest stop. Even in normal times, my system processes liquids faster than the average human. When the weather is cold or when I am really excited, I spend about as much time in the bathroom as I spend out of it. Well, the weather was cold on December 15th. And I know now that... no matter how calm I may act... I don't get much more excited than when my boys die. I was constantly thirsty... gulping coffee and orange juice and whatever helping hands were pushing at me. And... ten minutes later... I was having to excuse myself for a visit to the smallest room in the house.

On one of my first visits to the bathroom, I noticed a matchbook lying next to a scented candle on the back of the toilet. The matchbook was one that Kay and I had brought home from a visit to a Holiday Inn somewhere. The hotel's slogan stared up at me in white letters on a green background: "A better place to be."

I stared at the words for a long time. Eventually, I placed that matchbook in front of Tim and Don's pictures on my chest of drawers. I didn't consider the matchbook to be any kind of mysterious message from heavenly realms. Yet, the words *a better place to be* were soothing to me. They helped... and my advice to you is to take your soothing and encouragement wherever you can get them.

Another set of words reached out from the car radio in those early days of grief. The closing line of the popular song, *Starry, Starry Night* seemed made for the moment. It's a song in praise of Vincent Van Gogh and the beauty of his painting. The song's final line describes the frustrations with the work-a-day world that ultimately drove Van Gogh to suicide. Though I did not suspect any possibility of suicide in the boys' deaths, I *was* comforted by the singer's final words: "I could have told you, Vincent, this world was never meant for one as beautiful as you."

To my mind, it was a line that fit Tim and Don perfectly. They were creative, idealistic, sensitive. They were not going to fit easily into the work-a-day world. "Perhaps," I told myself, "the other side of death is *a better place to be*

29

for two kids who were facing rebuffs and uphill struggles as they tried to find their places in society." A matchbook cover. A pop song lyric. Take your consolation wherever you can find it.

Conversations and car trips at half speed... kidneys doing double time. The two days between the policeman's announcement and the boys' funeral seemed to last a week and a half! This distortion of time and reality is a good reason to obey a familiar bit of advice: "Don't ever try to make any important decisions while you are going through the grief process."

In retrospect, I have decided that... at least for the first three months of your grief... your mind is somewhere else. You walk. You talk. You sit up and take nourishment. You appear to be fully inhabiting your body. But... if someone had the power to look inside your skull... they would see a note on the kitchen table of your mind. The note would say, "Make yourself at home. I'll be back in three months."

5

TWO CEMENT BLOCKS, READY TO WEAR

There was another physical phenomenon that I could never have anticipated. It's that pair of invisible cement blocks that someone ties together and loops over your shoulders. Since they are invisible... and since they are so hard to describe... I have found that people rarely understand when I first begin to describe those blocks.

That is... people who have not *worn* the blocks find it hard to understand. People who have been through a grief process that involved the wearing of the blocks seem to know immediately and exactly what I am talking about. Very little description is required for them. They immediately nod their understanding.

If you are reading this book because of a recent life tragedy, you may well be wearing the block harness as you read these words.

But... for better or worse... for understanding or puzzlement... let me try to describe the two invisible cement blocks you get to wear as you begin your grief process. I use the term "cement blocks" for generic purposes. If all readers were from Nashville, where I grew up, I would refer to them as "Breeko Blocks." I suppose the local manufacturer of these 20-pound concrete blocks with the oval holes through them was the Breeko Company. I don't know how far and wide the Breeko Company sold its product. I only know that... if you said "Breeko Block" to a Nashville person... they would know exactly what you were talking about.

As I grew older and traveled more widely, I heard that same product referred to by many other brand names or regional names. In the part of the country where Kay grew up, they call them "cinder blocks." Other places, they are "concrete blocks." In spite of the fact that they have so many aliases, these blocks are one of the most universal building materials you will find. Around the world, they are a quick and economical way to build a wall.

Sometime very soon after learning of the boys' deaths... perhaps it was while I was standing in the shower trying to cry... invisible hands hung a pair of those invisible blocks over my shoulders. Even though I could not see the apparatus, it was easy to tell how it was made. Someone must have taken a length of invisible rope and threaded it through the holes of the invisible blocks. The resulting apparatus... though invisible... must look like two blocks on rope suspenders.

When the whole contraption is let down over your head, the ropes come to rest on your two shoulders and the length of the ropes is perfectly measured to assure that the two blocks will press in... from front and back... on your lungs. It is *possible* to breathe with the blocks on your shoulders... but not to breathe deeply.

As I say... it is virtually impossible to explain the invisible blocks and their harness to anyone who has not experienced the breathlessness of deep grief. People listen politely and respond courteously but they just don't get it.

On the other hand, you can begin explaining those blocks to a person who has been through the valley of the shadow of death and... no matter how clumsy your description may be... they are nodding in agreement and understanding almost immediately.

The blocks are not so heavy that you can't get up and move around but your legs and your lungs certainly know that... somewhere along the line... something new has been added. The result, of course, is that you tire easily but... more than anything else... you just can't take a deep breath. You want to... you think surely you must be able to... but there's just no room left in your chest cavity.

As the strange phenomenon continues with you day after day, you begin to wonder if this invisible boa constrictor is going to be a permanent fixture. How long are you going to be breathing with only the top tenth of your lung power? The answer in my experience is "three weeks." I wore my invisible block harness for a little over three weeks after the boys died. Then, it gradually got lighter and lighter.

Of course, not every grieving person gets a set of invisible cement blocks. Kay says she doesn't remember the shortness of breath as much as the constant *physical* tiredness that resulted from constant *emotional* exertion. She also remembers a major problem with focusing her concentration.

A friend told me that... after the sudden death of his wife... it was eighteen months before he could finish a book or sit through a whole television program. The *physical* evidences of your *emotional* pain may be shortness of breath... or tiredness... or something entirely different. Whatever it is... it's yours... it's right for you... and you need to stop fighting it and let it accomplish its purpose.

Someday, I intend to research the elapsed time for wearing grief blocks. I will check with people who have worn them and have felt them slowly melt away. I don't know how three weeks will stack up with the national average. Who knows? It might put me in the *Guinness Book of World Records* for the shortest or longest time for grief blocks to be worn.

I have no idea how I might place in the international ranking of building block averages (BBAs). I don't really care. This whole section of the story... with its ridiculous description of a preposterous concept... is intended to say to you that the grief that seems to be quite literally squeezing the life out of you... will ease. It is not forever. You will breathe *deeply* again... but it's going to take a little time.

For now, practice getting by on less air. You've got no business running any races for a while anyway. If it's not better around three weeks, let me know.

6

LET PEOPLE DO THINGS

Rob and Karen were the first of a long parade of loving "brothers and sisters" who would pass through our house in the hours, days, and weeks after the boys died. From the time Rob and Karen walked in our door until the time that the last person left must have been two weeks. During that time, we were never alone unless we wanted to be. We could go into a bedroom if we needed privacy. In the evenings, the crowd would thin out... the house would get quiet... Kay and I would excuse ourselves and go to bed for the night... with never a thought for locking doors or turning out lights.

The next morning, we would be awakened by the smells of coffee and the sounds of breakfast cooking. Someone had stayed the night. Someone else had arrived early with groceries to cook breakfast. Others would arrive to help us start another day. Throughout the day, people would come and go. There were soft drinks and food for all. People brought paper plates, paper towels, bags of ice, even a small refrigerator. Someone managed the kitchen. Someone answered the telephone. Someone kept lists of

who sent which flower arrangements. Someone else or-
ganized all those volunteers.

On that first morning... as Kay and I sat talking to a
visitor... one of the ladies came quietly up to Kay and said,
"I need to know where your sheets and pillow cases are
kept." Kay's automatic response was to say, "Oh, there's
no reason to worry about that kind of thing now." But the
lady said gently, "Kay, you have family coming from out of
town. If you'll show us where the linens are, we'll go ahead
and get the guest room ready." It's true the beds needed
to be changed. Equally important, that person needed to
change some sheets.

One of the things that people will do without being
asked is bring you food. We soon ran out of counter, table,
and refrigerator space to receive all the food that people
brought. So, we spread a continuous buffet and encouraged everyone who came in to fill a plate. Food helps
everybody. *We know what to do* when we have food in front
of us. A consoling visit is filled with uncertainties and
discomforts... filled with times when we don't know what
to do. A plate of food is a challenge we can handle.

We did something else that helped a lot. We asked one
of our friends to invite two or three couples to our house
for dinner each evening. You might assume that a dinner
party is the last thing you would enjoy in the early days of
grief. And yet... with the right people... sharing good food
and great memories of Tim and Don and Bryan... those
evening meals helped us a lot.

We were also fortunate to have a close friend who was
in the cemetery business. Because we knew that John was
a friend *first* and in the cemetery business *second*, he was
a tremendous help to us. At our request, he went along
when we went to make the wrenching decisions about
burial plots, coffins, and funeral services. You may not
have a friend in the cemetery business, but you certainly
have a friend who would love to help if you would just ask.

Pick someone who is not a member of your immediate family so that he or she is relatively objective and free of distorting emotions. Make it a person who can put good business sense into action. It's something he or she can *do*... when there is so little that can be done.

Let people drive you places. You may have been driving all your life. Driving yourself may even be tied to your feelings of independence and self-sufficiency. You may be an old hand at driving and doing three other things at the same time... but driving and grief don't mix.

In times of grief, your senses of speed and timing are distorted even when you think you are in full control. There is anger and hurt building up inside of you. Don't take that anger out into traffic. Let friends drive you for a while. It is something they know how to do. It helps them. It helps you. Let them take you when you need to go. Let them run errands when you don't need to go.

As our friends and relatives arrived at the airport... more than an hour away from our house on the other side of Atlanta... Kay and I never concerned ourselves with meeting their flights or providing transportation. Our friends gladly responded to any need. A two-hour round trip to the airport to meet a traveler you've never seen before is an inconvenient, uncomfortable, perhaps embarrassing assignment... but one that your friends will relish. They *need* to go to the airport. And you need to let them.

As I have heard more and more accounts from people who have been forsaken in their grief, I have become more and more appreciative of the church family that was so willing to share ours. These helpful people were not distant acquaintances dropping by to express formal condolences. They were our spiritual brothers and sisters... the spiritual aunts and uncles of three boys that had died. They were people who were hurting. They needed to be with us as much as we needed them.

If I could give one gift to every sufferer in the world, it would be the gift of an extended family of loving brothers and sisters. When we moved to Atlanta to become part of this church family, I had said that it seemed the kind of congregation where I wanted my boys to grow up. They did grow up there. And it was good for them. But somehow, it had never occurred to me that... if a church family is a good place to grow up... it's also a good place to die.

Our loving friends became our servants. They desperately needed to *do something*. Perhaps even more than Kay and I needed to be served, the members of our spiritual family needed to serve. As people come to see you, as they hold your hand, and as they search their minds for words to express their sympathy, there is one phrase that just pops out naturally. "If there's anything we can do, please call on us." They mean it sincerely. They really would like to get their flesh-and-blood hands around a tangible task that could help them feel like they are taking a swing at the terrible intangible helplessness they are feeling.

Not too many generations ago, there were actual jobs that people could do to physically work through their emotional and spiritual pain. Before backhoes and hired grave diggers, it was family and friends who went to the cemetery and dug the grave. A grave is a major piece of physical work. It's not a small hole for planting a shrub. It's a hole longer and deeper than you are tall. It's a long, hard, sweaty job. It's probably one the most blessed assignments that could be given an able-bodied friend of the deceased.

In our time, of course, grave digging is just another cost item on the invoice from the cemetery. It's done by a mechanical digger driven by a person who never knew the deceased. It's another of the healing activities that modern life has snatched out of the hands of people who desperately need to do those jobs. We need to swing a pick in anger at the ground. We need to stomp a shovel into the earth. We need to heave shovels full of dirt toward the top of the pile until the sweat rolls off of us. And we need to plop down on the dirt pile for a breather... and look up at trees and leaves and sky... and crumple a clod of dirt into dust between our fingers. We need to do those things to re-establish our perspective of life and death and dust unto dust... but mechanical wonders and marketing geniuses have stolen those opportunities away.

Only a few months before our boys died, our church family had lost another of its children. Jim and Jan's beautiful, blond fourteen-year-old daughter had succumbed to a sudden respiratory attack. Jodi died in the car as her mother was trying to get her to the hospital. Like many others, Kay and I went to Jim and Jan's house as soon as we heard. We didn't know what to say or do... but we knew we needed to be there. There were lots of people standing around talking and trying to explain the unexplainable to each other.

Kay and I talked with Jim and Jan for a while... proving repeatedly that we had absolutely no idea what to say. We hugged them, turned them over to the next folks in line, and walked into the kitchen where the soft drinks and cakes and cookies were arriving faster than they could be eaten. Within a few moments, I had talked as much as I could stand and... when I noticed that the dishes were piling up next to the sink... I jumped at the task. I didn't know how to explain Jodi's death... but I knew how to wash dishes. I needed to do something... anything... that felt like it was for Jim and Jan.

We stayed a while. I finished the dishes. We stayed longer. I wandered out into the carport. The grass in the backyard looked like it needed to be mowed. I found the lawnmower, started it up, and mowed the grass. I didn't know how to explain Jodi's death... but I knew how to mow grass. I needed to do something... anything... that felt like it was for Jim and Jan.

When our boys died and a little group of us sat in our den and watched the December morning turn from darkness to daylight, Bud finally said, "I'm cooking breakfast." I had known Bud for twenty-eight years and had never known him to cook anything except a shrewd business deal. Bud was the last person in the house that any of us would have nominated to cook breakfast. And... while there may have been a few expressions of amazement... there was not one person who questioned the sentiment. Bud needed to *do* something... anything... that felt like it was for Charlie and Kay and Bob and Carole.

When people come to you and say, "If there's anything we can do, please call on us," listen to their offers as sincerely as they are making them. They really want to do something. They can't explain the thing that is hurting you so much but they would sincerely love to do something... anything... that feels like it is for you.

Let them do things for you. Don't burden yourself trying to be creative in thinking up clever little jobs to keep all your friends occupied with busy work. Your primary job is to get yourself through this time of loss. Take care of yourself first. But, when you do think of little jobs that need to be tended to and people that need to be contacted, take your friends up on their offers to help. They asked. They meant it. Let them do it.

Don't let your pride convince you that you need to be independent and never beholden to anyone. You will go through this alone... but you'll go through it alone better if you let people help. It will help you and it will help them if you can give *the gift of asking*. People need to do things and you... need to let them.

7

PEOPLE ARE GOING TO SAY
A LOT OF DUMB STUFF

It was a while before we were able to piece together the scenario in which the boys died. The policeman went strictly by the book and... in true Joe Friday style... gave us "nothing but the facts." The result was that... for the first few hours... our imaginations dealt with even more frightening possibilities than they needed to. All we had been told was that the deaths seemed to be caused by "a combination of things."

A combination of *what* things? My mind raced through lurid scenes of drug or alcohol experimentation with all the inherent possibilities of accidental, but fatal, mixtures. I even thought of teenage suicide pacts like the ones that had recently been in the news a lot. The simple fact was that *we did not know* how they had died. In retrospect, I realize that the things you *don't* know about the death of your loved one will always be ten times harder to deal with than the things you *do* know.

The county policeman who had broken the news at Bob and Carole's house had been a bit more gentle in his delivery. He was, it turned out, a man who had a teenage son of his own and he perhaps transgressed department policy as he enclosed Bob and Carole in a bear hug as he broke the news to them. He also gave them more information about the probable cause of death.

He told them that the cause of death was almost certainly carbon monoxide from a leak in the car's exhaust system. The boys had spent Sunday afternoon at the mall, seeing and being seen. They had stopped by our house to get a couple of aspirin for Bryan's headache. And they had left our house, we assumed, on the way to Sunday evening church services.

Evidently, they had stopped on the way and that's where the "combination of things" came in. The police had found a couple of aerosol canisters of canned air... freon under aerosol pressure... used by commercial artists to blow dust off of photographic slides and eraser shavings off of drawings. Tim had fashioned a length of rubber tubing and a homemade face mask into a device for inhaling the freon.

All my life, I had heard of kids sniffing glue for a momentary high... but freon was a new one on me. In the time since the boys died, we have been told by several young people that sniffing freon is a relatively common practice. It's cheap, it's legal, and from the description of one youngster, "It's not much of a high."

We gradually pieced together the scene. Bryan was in the back seat. Bryan... who had a reputation as "Mr. Clean"... the absolute last person who would have experimented with any kind of drugs or alcohol... would have just taken the two aspirin and laid his head back on the seat to wait for his headache to ease. Tim and Don in the front seat turned their favorite cassette tape up full blast, took a deep breath of freon, and leaned back to float for a moment. Because it was winter and because his car was sometimes hard to start, Tim left the motor running.

Hours later, after midnight, a policeman found the car with the motor still running. The boys were all in their places with their seat belts fastened. The policeman thought that they had gone to sleep... as indeed they had. The medical report ruled the cause of death as carbon monoxide poisoning. There were traces of freon found in Tim and Don's systems... nothing in Bryan's.

The weeks around Christmas are notoriously slow news times. The story of the boys' deaths went straight to the front page of the paper and ran as the top story on all the television channels. It was a story with appeal for editors and producers. It involved teenagers... and lots of people had teenagers. It involved carbon monoxide... and lots of teenagers drive old cars. And there were those mysterious aerosol cans found in the car. Public interest in the ominous "combination of things" was almost a certainty.

If you've had your story told by the media, you've probably come to appreciate the imperfect nature of those who report the news. They are always in a hurry to do the story and, therefore, working from preliminary reports and impressions. They are eager to make the story simple and, therefore, in constant danger of jumping to unwarranted conclusions. They are not emotionally involved or concerned with the feelings of family or close friends. And... if they make a mistake or an unfair inference in their accounts... you can be sure that corrections never get the same emphasis that the original story does.

If your tragedy is one that has attracted the attention of the news media, there is one thing to remember: You never successfully argue with the media or straighten them out when they make reporting errors. To try to do so only creates their follow-up stories. Your best procedure for

43

surviving the media is to understand their motivations, understand their deadlines, and don't give them anything. When they call... be polite... but don't tell them anything.

Of course, the news media are not the only ones who will hurt you with their words. Ordinary, run-of-the-mill human beings... like your own friends and family... have the ability to wound with their words and insinuations. People seem to have an inherent need to *place blame*. When something goes wrong, we have a built-in compulsion to identify and point the finger at whoever has caused it to go wrong. We want to *fix* things and... when there can be no fixing... as in the case of a death... our fixing urge unfortunately can be satisfied with a bit of reckless finger-pointing.

It's rarely finger-pointing with intent to cause pain. It just grows out of the fact that... when there's a death... people stand around a lot. They stand around and they talk. And... when they run out of facts to talk about... they express opinions. And before they know it, opinions have come tumbling out of their mouths, been confirmed by the absent-minded nods of listeners, and taken on the status of approved concepts... concepts approved to be repeated and eventually to harden into facts.

This process of theories hardening into facts happens a lot within grieving families. If Dad dies of a heart attack, grown children may whisper angrily to each other that Mom drove him to it by the way she made demands all those years. They don't really believe it... but there is something soothing about identifying a culprit.

Of course, Mom is dealing with her own load of self-imposed guilt and the last thing she needs is to sense that others are pointing at her as the cause of this tragedy. We are harder on ourselves than anyone else can ever be. When any child dies, guilt comes to live with that child's parents. Reasonable or not, grieving people are magnets for guilt.

Assigning blame is a reflex reaction that has driven permanent wedges into many a family. So, be prepared. You may hear people verbalizing words or insinuations that you know they cannot really believe. Try to understand that they are grasping at straws... looking for someone to blame for pain that really is nobody's fault.

If your tragedy happens to get into the newspapers or on television, you can also anticipate hearing from absolute strangers who take it on themselves to explain to you the moral of your tragedy. Kooks who have no personal knowledge of you or your behavior may drop you a card or letter to explain that God wouldn't have brought this tragedy upon you if you had been *living right*. They will further suggest that this whole thing was sent into your life for the purpose of bringing you to repentance.

It is, of course, the ultimate presumption for anyone to speak for God and equally unwise to make judgments about people they've never even met. Furthermore, there is a basic flaw in their logic: if God were indeed zapping all who sin, there would be no one left standing! You only survive such messages from strangers by shaking your head and being amazed at the kind of folks who are waiting in the woodwork, reading their papers, and making themselves feel more important by rushing forward to stomp your heart as it lies unprotected on the ground.

Equally common is another group who rush forward with spiritual advice. They mean well and their advice is the kind that you will automatically thank them for... but find impossible to actually follow. Their favorite set of words is, "Just turn it over to the Lord."

Who can argue with such advice? If you have had even the loosest association with religion, those words sound like a pronouncement of faith... words that no one could question. Don't they describe what a true believer would do? Shouldn't we be able to turn our burdens over to the Lord and walk away from them? Of course not.

The one time that it is recorded that Jesus wept, he was at a funeral. He certainly had faith in God. He knew God's power over death. He even knew that he was about to restore the dead man to life. Yet, he wept. And again... on the night before his own death... Jesus agonized over the ordeal he knew he would endure. The Bible's description of the sweat rolling off Jesus "like great drops of blood" is quite unlike the naive insinuation of those who want you to "turn it over to the Lord" and carry on like a picture of inspirational peace and composure.

Faith in God's ultimate control over all that happens has been one of the things that has enabled Kay and me to make it through the long and drawn out process of grief and resumption of life. But it is insensitive and unrealistic for a well-wisher to propose to a grieving person that... because God is all powerful... they should not continue to grieve. Sadness, despair, rage, loneliness – even moments of vengeful fantacies – are as natural as God's creation.

At a time when there are no words... "Just turn it over to the Lord" sounds like it ought to be quite a helpful line. It wasn't for us. We smiled and said "Thanks" but we would not have relieved ourselves of the pain and the hurting if we could have. Part of us had died and it seemed the most natural thing in the world to hurt... to hurt unbearably... to hurt with a pain that could not be taken away.

The reason that people are going to say so many dumb things to you as you grieve is that *there are no words* that help. Most people yearn to help. They open their mouths and let words out... words that are automatic, unexamined, and untried. The best thing you can do for yourself... and for your long-term relationship with those who seek to comfort... is to turn off the sound. Just as if you were watching them on television and could lean forward and turn the volume down to zero. The important thing for you is the picture. You need to see that they have come. They have come with pain on their faces. They have come with faces yearning to speak comfort. These are pictures you need to see... but turn off the sound.

Of course, you *cannot* turn off the sound. Your ears are working... no matter how much you might wish they were not. You do hear what they say and... in the long run... you will be glad. You will be glad because... after those dumb statements have rolled off their tongues... you can consciously decide to hear *what they were trying to communicate*... rather than *what they say*.

There is one other reason to keep the sound turned up and listen to what people are saying as they try to comfort you. Someone... maybe several someones... will say something you will be glad you heard. It may be the person from whom you least expect eloquence. It may be a child. It may even be a statement with no intended consolation. The one that comes to mind for me is something said by one of Don's friends who is also named Don. As he talked with Kay and me about the great times he and our Don had had together, he said, "We got to thinking so much alike, that sometimes we couldn't decide which one of us was Don... and which one was the other Don!"

We remember with pleasure things people shared with us about our *living* boys. We had to filter the things they tried to explain about our *dead* boys. When trying to comfort, it's better to talk about what we know. We know about living. We are yet to understand the circumstances that follow life.

8

EVERY HUG DILUTES THE PAIN

If there is one method of communication that *does* work in times of grief, it is the hug. The comfort content of words is hit or miss... but sincere hugs always make clear statements.

I grew up in a family that did not express its affection with lots of hugs and kisses. As I left home and encountered other families' ways of doing things, I liked what I saw in families that hugged a lot. As Kay and I dated and planned the home we would establish, we committed to being huggers... to frequently and physically demonstrate our affection for each other. For us, it has been a good principle upon which to build a life.

As our friends visited our home on the day we learned about the boys' deaths, there were many hugs. A hug finds its own length and level of intensity depending on the relationship you have with the person who approaches. If you have known them long and well... or... if you know without a word being spoken that they have suffered a deep personal loss in the departure of your loved one... the hug may go on and on. You may deposit tears on each other's shoulders. No words need be uttered for volumes to be communicated.

Among our friends, I was surprised to discover two world class huggers. One was a six-foot-five leader in our church. Dick and I had been friends but never huggers. But Dick has two sons and... when he walked into our house on that cold December 15th... there was no small talk. I was probably reaching for a handshake when Dick took me into his arms and nearly squeezed the life out of me. Not a word was spoken but his long arms were clearly wrapped around me... around my boys... and around his boys too. He squeezed me until the tears came. It felt wonderful. I must tell him that his hug continues to make a difference for me even to this day.

The other world class hugger I discovered was a woman that Kay and I had met when we first moved to Atlanta. Lois was just out of college and a part of the active campus group at our church. She became a close friend and an honorary aunt during the years our boys were growing up. When Lois walked into our house on that December 15th, I got one of the best hugs of my life. All her grief transferred itself into physical strength that sent crackling noises up and down my spinal column. Great hugging is a gift.

A hug says, "I am a child again. I am just like I was before I learned all these words that we use to talk. I am hurting for me. I am hurting for you. There are no words to express the frustration we share at this moment. Please, just hold me. Hold me quietly... and let our spirits do the talking."

There is no way to *quantify* the pain that you are facing as you read these words. Pain doesn't come in pounds or ounces or gallons. You just feel like you are standing before a mountain that you are going to have to move one spoonful at a time. It is a task you can never hope to complete... a mountain that you can never hope to finish moving. But... as you stand surveying that mountain of grief... a loved one steps forward with a hug that communicates clearly. You can almost picture that person stepping up to your mountain of grief with a shovel and saying, "I cannot move the mountain for you... but I will take this one shovel full of your grief and deal with it myself."

It seemed to me that every hug helped to dilute the pain a little more... that every sincere hugger carried away a small quantity of the mountain Kay and I were facing. In the time since our boys died, I have had several occasions to visit funeral homes, feeling a sincere desire to communicate the depth of my concern for a long-time friend. The most natural thing in the world in such a case is for me to wrap that person in a hug... and usually... I hear words coming out of my mouth: "Let me have a little of the mountain." Those are not words that are likely to mean a thing to the griever. The words are for me. The hug is for the griever.

When our boys died, I didn't usually give people a choice about whether they were going to be huggers or not. At the funeral home, people I had not seen in years would come cautiously forward to express their condolences. It was easy to see the question marks on their faces. "What do I say?" "What do I do?" "Why did I talk myself into coming to this funeral home, anyway?"

While they were still wondering how familiar to be, I would grab them and give them a hug. One guy that I had worked with many years before showed up at the funeral home and was obviously ill at ease. He was completely unprepared for the joy and appreciation I felt at seeing him walk through the door. I immediately remembered the friendship we had built through many a lunch time conversation when we worked together. He had probably hoped he could sneak in, sign the guest book, and sneak out. He never had a chance. The hugging machine grabbed him... a friendship was instantly reestablished... and the healing communication flowed.

Whether that friend wanted it or not, I gave him a hug full of my grief to take away and work on. There were lots of friends who came with their shovel-sized hugs and a willingness to help us work on the mountain. There were others who weren't sure why they were coming but I grabbed them, gave them a hug, and gave them a shovel full of our grief mountain to take home with them.

Every hug helps to dilute the pain... to move the mountain. Don't be selfish with your mountain. Don't be a martyr about your grief. There is plenty of mountain to keep you busy for the rest of your life... and... if your friends hadn't been willing to help... they wouldn't have showed up with those spoons and shovels and hugs.

9

EVERYONE ELSE'S FIRST TIME

I often think about the policeman who broke the news to us. It was a terrible assignment he had been given and he did the best he knew how. There must be a better way. Maybe the training he had been given was based on the idea that the person is about to receive a shock anyway and one giant shock is better than revealing the information gradually. I suppose there are advantages both ways but... if I ever have to break bad news again... I intend to do it a little at a time.

Among support groups of people who have lost loved ones, there are some unbelievable stories about the clumsiness and insensitivity of public servants breaking bad news. The worst I've heard was from a person who received a phone call that said, "This is the city coroner's office. I am prohibited by law from telling you over the phone why I am calling but it might be a good idea for you to come down to our office. It is located at - - -."

I should be much more understanding of our policeman's bluntness and inability to break news gently because... within a few hours of his announcement... I was standing with my oldest son, Rick, in the lobby of his place of employment and failing miserably to break news gently.

Maybe there is no *good* way to deliver *bad* news. But... if I am ever in that position again... there are three things I intend to do. One, I will escort the person to a place where he or she can be alone to receive the news. Two, I will have them sit down. Three, I will introduce the subject of tragedy before I tell them the details of the specific tragedy.

I will start with, "Something terrible has happened." I believe I would rather let the person's imagination run slightly ahead of my words... perhaps even guessing worse things than I am about to reveal... than to drop the whole load of bricks on them with one giant, unexpected crash.

Of course, it is easy to describe in step-by-step fashion the things we *intend* to do in an emergency. When the real time comes, those good intentions may be completely neutralized by the shock we are in at the time. I assumed that breaking the bad news to Rick was one of the things I needed to do personally... part of my role as the strong father figure. In retrospect, I can see that it might have been better for all of us if I had swallowed that pride and asked someone to help me do that... someone who was not in shock at the time.

As the funeral, the burial, and the kindnesses of friends gradually become history, you move into the stage in which you will spend the rest of your life: the *long-term* processing of your grief. This stage bears a remarkable resemblance to the second and third days following major surgery. The anesthesia begins to wear off and you begin to realize just how much the wound really hurts.

In the creator's wisdom, our minds are designed to go into shock when a loved one dies. Our circuits blow. When there are things too awful to be considered, the brain mercifully lets them pass through without seriously processing them. In the coming years, you will probably look back on what you are going through today and realize that... even when you thought you were right on top of things... your mind was on hold.

One friend... whose son died recently... shared with me that he keeps getting lost in familiar territory. This is a successful businessman who has been making his way around the world for years. And yet, he finds himself driving in an area that he knows quite well and suddenly realizes that... while everything around him looks familiar... he has absolutely no idea where he is or how to get where he is trying to go. At first, he came to the conclusion that is often embraced by those in the early stages of grief... that he was simply losing his mind. But... as time passed... he found that the frequency and degree of his getting lost were diminishing. And... though he is still too close to his son's death to believe it... the time will come when he will function as efficiently as ever. Even before that, he will face the unexpected trauma of sharing other peoples' first times to hear the news.

You ease back into your daily schedule. You return to work or to school or to the super market. You encounter an old friend or an associate who has not heard about the tragedy that has entered your life. That's when you realize as never before that our society's conversational small talk is crisscrossed with emotional land mines. "How's the family?" "How are the kids?" "What are those youngsters of yours up to now?"

In some cases, it is easy to perform a little conversational slight of hand and get past the questions without opening a topic that you know will be hard to close. But... in other cases... there is no way to avoid pulling the pin on an emotional hand grenade and tossing it into the middle of the conversation.

So, you tell them what happened. Perhaps, it is the first time you have put it into words. You have thought about nothing else for days but you have never before heard the description coming out of your own mouth. Words that you assumed you could say without a cracking voice get stuck in your throat. You cough. You clear your throat. You get misty eyed.

Eventually, you get the words out there... and you wish you hadn't. Your conversational partner is crushed. You are suddenly watching him or her deal with the very first moment of hearing of the news. For them, you have become the county policeman who has... without preamble or warning... stopped their hearts in mid-beat.

They are shocked. They are embarrassed. They are sorry they asked. They feel guilty for asking the most innocent and commonplace of questions. They feel like brutes for causing you to speak of it. They don't know what to say or do. And... right before your experienced eyes... they begin to replay the days and weeks you have just gone through and hoped never to see again.

As the months and years pass, the emotional trauma of this situation begins to diminish... but you never get over the dread that... when you make a new acquaintance... they are about to ask the question that will subject them to answers they don't want to hear. You always dread the occasion that may force you to watch someone else go through it for the first time.

The answers you learn to give may, at first, give you the feeling that you are denying your own children... that they have ceased to have importance to you by dying. In the earliest days... when someone asked me how many children I had... I was confronted with the *partial* truth that I had one son... or... the *full* truth that I had three sons. The partial truth protected my associate from embarrassment but left me feeling like a traitor to Tim and Don. The full truth was likely to be followed with questions that would pull the pin on that conversational hand grenade.

Now... after going through the experience again and again... I have learned to adapt my response to the person doing the asking. If it is a passing acquaintance and the question is a mere social courtesy with no real desire for information or personal involvement, I tell them about Rick... and smile inwardly as I picture Tim and Don laughing at the idea of Rick being an only child.

On the other hand... if I sense that the person asking about the family has a sincere interest in getting to know me and what makes me tick... I trot out the whole gang... Rick, Tim, and Don... and explain that Tim and Don were killed in an accident when they were 22 and 19.

There is no way for a caring person to hear that kind of information without shock. But the way that I deliver that information communicates to the person whether my life and personality came to an absolute halt and have never progressed beyond the moment of the boys' deaths... or... whether their deaths are an inescapable and undeniable part of me and... if you want to know me... you need to know about this event that shaped my life.

Tim and Don's deaths are *part* of me... but they are not the *end* of me.

10

INEVITABLE GUILT

The more people I talk to who have lost loved ones, the more I think that feelings of guilt are automatic. Guilt is a natural consequence of being human and suffering a loss. It is one of the steps we go through as we struggle back toward reality. As our minds go over and over the story... trying to find some way to comprehend it... there inevitably emerges a conviction that... at least in part... we *caused* the death... or... *contributed* to the conditions that caused the death.

Of course, there are some people who *are* guilty... people who were actual participants in accidents that took the lives of their loved ones. I have listened to them tell about tragic hunting accidents. I have shuddered as they described backing the car over a toddler in the driveway. I have watched tears fill a handkerchief as a parent spoke of firm discipline that she feared might have driven her child to suicide.

On the other hand, I have listened to the guilt stories of people who were clearly not guilty. Though they were nowhere near when their loved ones died, they beat themselves up for failing to have influence they think they should have had... or failing to take actions they think they should have taken... influences and actions that might... just might... have kept the horrible thing from happening.

I have heard the stories of those who are guilty. I have heard the guilt stories of those who are not guilty. It seems to me that the actuality of the guilt is neither here nor there. The difference lies in the way the person chooses to deal with the guilt... whether it be real or imagined. If you want to punish yourself daily for the tragic thing that happened, you will almost certainly be able to find something in the situation that will allow you to take the blame. Or... if you can see that accidents happen... that all accidents are *freak* accidents... and that yesterday is not today... then you can look guilt in the eye and keep on living.

Tim and Don and Bryan's deaths gave me an immediate and long-term guilt battle to fight. The boys died in a car that had a faulty muffler. I knew Tim's car had a faulty muffler and I didn't get it fixed. Every time Tim would drive up to our house in that car that sounded like a tank, I would repeat a familiar sequence of thoughts and actions. First, I would be embarrassed for the neighbors to hear that car and know that it was still in our driveway. Then, I would think about getting the muffler fixed. Then, I would remind myself that it was Tim's car and Tim's responsibility. I would talk to Tim about it. He would assure me that he was planning to get it fixed right away... as soon as he got a check in the mail for some work he had done.

Next day... same loud muffler... another talk with Tim... another promise. It was obvious to me that the muffler was not high on Tim's list of priorities. It was equally obvious to me that Tim was 22 years old and the last thing he needed was a father who kept bailing him out by tending to things that Tim needed to do for himself. I made a conscious, intentional decision not to do Tim's job for him... not to replace the muffler on Tim's car... the muffler that eventually killed Tim and Don and Bryan.

You can see that... if I wanted to shirk my responsibility for continuing on with life... if I wanted to give up trying... I could greet every rising sun with the memory of a long-past December 15th. I could build a pedestal in the back yard and place Tim's faulty muffler on top of it. I could bow to that monument each morning... and pay it respect as the reason I ought to be forgiven for giving up and not trying any more.

It would be a ridiculous sight for the neighbors to watch me come out each morning to bow down to the Great Muffler Monument. But it would be no more ridiculous than some of the presumptions of guilt to which grieving people often surrender. Whether you are actually guilty of a mistake that brought about a death... or... whether you are going through the natural human exploration of all the "what ifs" that might have changed your story... don't surrender to guilt. You cannot avoid guilt... but you can keep from surrendering to it.

Every time my guilt raises its seductive head, I have to remind myself that... given the same situation again... I would make the same decisions. I would refrain from replacing the muffler on a car that Tim had committed to take care of himself. I would be embarrassed for the neighbors to hear the car that sounded like a tank, but I would think it more important for Tim that I *not* fix the muffler.

Of course, I will never be "given the same situation again." I readily admit to abandoning the teacher role and jumping in to fix lots of things on Rick's car since the accident in which his two younger brothers died. That was then. This is now.

A lot of Bible verses have taken on new meaning for me since the boys died. The one verse that has come to mean the most to me is the verse where Jesus tells his audience in the sermon on the mount, "Judge not, that you be not judged." Before the boys died, that verse said to me "Don't be critical and condemning of other people because that's a good way to keep them from criticizing you."

Since the boys died... I have come to see the divine wisdom of the two central words... *judge not.* I have realized that none of us humans is in a position to accurately pass judgment on the guilt or innocence of anyone... especially ourselves. We know only a smattering of the full story and even the parts that we do know are seen through the tunnel vision of our own limited perspectives.

It's a waste of my time to judge... to condemn... to pass sentence... on any person involved in the boys' deaths. On Tim. On Don. On Bryan. On Charlie. I have no right to judge. I have inadequate data by which to judge. I have everything to lose... and nothing to gain... by passing judgment... even on myself.

11

ALL THAT STUFF

Don's room in our house contained the normal amount of junk for an average American teenager. Tim's area was an absolute rat's nest. We had often joked that we never allowed anyone to venture into Tim's room without a tetanus shot.

Until the boys died, it had never occurred to me how much stuff we humans accumulate and how totally useless the majority of it is to anyone else. Neither had I realized that... when someone dies... someone else has to deal with each and every piece of that stuff. It is more than a chore. It is a chore with an emotional booby trap attached to each and every tiny piece.

I sat and listened one evening as a group of parents who had lost children discussed the subject of getting rid of the stuff. The opinions of the group were evenly divided. Some said that clearing out their child's stuff immediately after the death was the smartest thing they had done. The others were glad they had kept the child's room as a virtual shrine for several years and... only after the passage of time... begun to dispose of a few of the things at a time.

It was a polite conversation about a subject of mutual interest. But consider the potential conflict and pain that await when one grieving parent wants to keep every beloved memento and the other grieving parent wants to clear things out. That's the point at which both must remember that *people are more important than things.* Decisions about temporary stuff are far less important than the permanent relationships between the grieving decision makers.

Stuff is just stuff. *You* are the factor that turns it into either treasure or trash. If you are the kind of person who can relive happy moments by touching and feeling the objects of those moments, then you probably will do well to let the stuff stay exactly as it is. Create a museum where you can be reminded of every small detail of your loved one's life. If it works for you, install a little velvet rope across the doorway of that person's room and keep it for your own private chapel. One mother told me that her favorite times are when she can send the rest of the family off to the mall, go into her daughter's room, sit among her little girl's things, turn the pages of her scrapbook, and cry her eyes out.

I am at the other extreme when it comes to stuff. I don't believe that I ever really identified my boys with their clothes or toys or other stuff. I saw the kids as entities very separate from all that transient paraphernalia. That's probably more likely to be true in a family where much of the stuff was always being handed down. It's a little hard to think of that brown sweater as representing one of the boys since it was first Rick's brown sweater, then Tim's brown sweater, then Don's brown sweater.

I have heard grieving parents tell about the enjoyment and memories they can bring back by smelling their kids' clothes and recalling them through their distinctive odors... both pleasant and unpleasant. Neither my sense of smell nor my memory are that good... but more important in my case... is the fact that I just can't stand to see that brown sweater sit year after year in a drawer when there are people who need it to protect them from the cold. To me, I can best honor Tim and Don by putting their things to use... letting those things live and accomplish their purposes.

Not long before our boys died, I had talked with a long-time friend whose husband had recently died. She told me that someone had given her the advice that "as soon as possible" she should sort through all of her husband's things and dispose of the ones she wasn't going to keep. She had followed that advice and was very glad she had. "Every day that passed would have made it harder to let anything go," she told me.

That lady's advice was the only thing I had ever heard on the subject when our boys died. I didn't know there was any other way to do it. So, I took the advice. For me, it turned out to be the right advice. For several weeks, I was going through stuff... a phenomenal volume of stuff... stuff from all kinds of sources... stuff that gave me some good memories... and stuff that made me furious.

There were, of course, some things we did keep. A piece of furniture that Don loved now sits in our guest room with his favorite trophies and mementos on it. We saved some of Tim's stuff too... including a sewing cabinet he bought at an estate sale as a present for Kay. He stripped the finish off but never got around to refinishing the piece. For now, that sewing cabinet sits in pieces in our attic. Some day, I intend to finish that job for Tim. But... beyond a few things that were uniquely Tim or Don... the rest of it was just stuff... miles and miles of stuff.

The clothes were the easy part. Once they were unwound from around the legs of beds, reclaimed from the bottomless pit in the back of the closet, dug out from behind the books on the shelves, and run through the heavy duty cycle of the washing machine, there turned out to be more clothes than either Tim or Don would ever have believed they owned. Tim had 35 T-shirts... each with its own emblazoned message... each with its own memory. Once cleaned, the clothes were easy to sort... easy to find homes for... easy to let go.

Only recently did Rick reveal to me that... in my zeal to clothe the homeless... I had also scooped up several of his shirts and several of his friend's shirts. They had been in Tim's room and had gone out the door to clothe the homeless right along with Tim and Don's clothes.

The items that bothered me the most were the things that did not *belong* to us but had been accumulated through the years. I returned stacks of library books to various schools our boys had attended. I returned a sack of football equipment to one of the local high schools. Don had proudly added to his room's decor one of those folding safety barricades that road construction crews put out. Since there was no designation of ownership on it, I folded it up, put it in the back of the car, stopped in the middle of a stretch of road under construction, and left it sitting there with others of its kind... its light flashing happily as though it had never been kidnapped.

Both Tim and Don were active in play production and theater... Don as a natural performer... and Tim... the boy who could make almost anything... as a promising costume and set designer. Set designers must, of course, be pack rats. They have to be the kind of people who can always imagine a second life for anything you are about to throw away. Tim's collection of potential treasures had already filled the loft of our A-frame house and a sizable part of the attic. By the time I had sorted through, categorized, and boxed it all, we were able to donate nearly a thousand dollars worth of lighting, costumes, make-up, paints, construction materials, and promising scraps to a local theater company. They were treasures to Tim... trash to me... and treasures again to the theater manager to whom I delivered them.

For me... it works best for those things to be living and working. Today, I do not remember Tim and Don because of the stuff of their pasts. I remember them every time I hear about another play in production... or... drive through another road construction area and see a hundred safety barricades winking at me. "Hi, Dad... Remember me?"

There is a piece of advice that has to be mentioned at the end of these thoughts about all that stuff. I am told that far less than half the people in our society have made wills. And... if we were to speak only of single people under 30... there would be almost none who had wills. Their assumptions are that, number one, they are not going to die, and, number two, they don't have anything worth anything. I would have probably agreed on both counts... until I had to try to legally dispose of two cars which were titled in Tim's and Don's names. I had to get legal authority to close out their meager bank accounts. I even had to be legally approved to pay off some minor debts they had incurred. If they had had even the simplest one-page wills, a couple of my weeks of dealing with all their stuff would have been greatly eased.

A will seems a cold and impersonal thing to mention in a discussion of the more emotional aspects of grief. And yet, one of the most common emotional problems any bereaved person faces... be it a grieving parent, a widow, or grown children settling an estate... is anger toward the departed for leaving things in such a mess.

One of the small tasks I accomplished in the weeks after the boys died, was to get Rick to a lawyer's office and get a simple will drawn up for him. There is never a pleasant time to tend to such a somber duty, but each of us needs to do it as a favor to those we love who are going to be standing knee-deep in our stuff after we have gone.

On a more long term basis, I have come to see my own collection of stuff quite differently since the boys died. I look at some of the things that I have been keeping around and I can almost hear the comments as Kay and Rick are sorting through it all. "What value could Dad possibly have seen in this thing?" "Just look at this! Isn't it just like him to be saving this?"

Without doubt... one of the benefits of our inevitable brushes with death is that we momentarily get our thinking clarified about our possessions. We are reminded once again that: we are separate from the things that belong to us. We are not our stuff. The bumper stickers that praise "dying with the most toys" are just short-sighted. We will all go through the door... our stuff stays here.

12

DISASTER INTENSIFIES WHAT'S ALREADY THERE

Sometime during your period of grieving... possibly when you need it least... someone is going to feel compelled to share with you the horrifying statistics about the frequency of divorce among parents who lose children or of suicide among those who lose spouses. It's just as well that I can't remember any of the exact numbers because *general* stats don't mean a thing in your *specific* life... and... the stat makers keep changing them all the time anyway.

Suffice it to say that the statistics *do* show an alarming frequency in divorces... and other life upheavals... in the months following the death of a loved one. And it might be easy to look at those numbers and conclude that your previously happy marriage is suddenly doomed to fall apart... adding insult to the life injury you have already sustained. That conclusion is not necessarily so. In fact, the opposite may occur.

The experience that Kay and I have had... and experiences shared with me by other sufferers... bring me to the conclusion that the death of a loved one does not cause divorce. Rather, it *intensifies* whatever marriage relationship existed prior to the tragedy. In our case, the marriage relationship was based on absolute commitment and better-than-average communication. Neither of us would call it a perfect marriage and we've certainly had our rough spots through the years. But... because we have both sincerely wanted the best possible marriage... we have developed an honesty of communication that enabled us to keep talking through the relationship pitfalls that naturally accompany the grief process.

One of the most common trouble spots for couples arises from the fact that no two people go about the grieving process in exactly the same way. And since no two people have the same ways of dealing with grief... it is almost inevitable that there will be friction. One father told me, "My wife thought I didn't care about our child's death because I wasn't crying all the time like she was. Little did she know that I cried all the way to work and all the way home. But, around the house, I felt like I had to be strong for the family."

Another friction point built into the marriage relationship has to do with the temptation to *blame* somebody for the death. Frustration and anger make us want to hurt somebody... and who is handier than a spouse! The differences in our communication styles contribute to the confusion. One spouse wants to *solve* problems. The other wants to *discuss* problems. Action people and discussion people are destined for communication conflict. And... when the communication is literally a matter of life and death... the conflict has the potential of destroying the relationship.

Irony strikes again in life: the thing that the relationship needs most is the thing that the two partners feel least like doing. They need to talk. They need to say what they are feeling even if it makes little sense at the time. They need to express the things that they *do* know... the love that supersedes the disaster... the determination to be patient and understanding even when the other's behavior is frustrating. Communicating is the last thing the injured partners feel like doing... and the one thing they need most to nourish the relationship that can enable them to survive.

When the lost loved one is not a child but a spouse, the survivor can still go through a one-sided version of the communication breakdown. I have listened to widows who were furious with their departed husbands for the habits or the behaviors that brought on their deaths. Because the departed one is not around to argue, the survivor can make a strong, unanswerable case. There is, however, no consolation in winning a one-sided argument. The anger is not abated. The sadness is increased.

The positive side of this whole idea is that a disaster also intensifies the good things about relationships. Marriage partners who have gone through the fire together share a bond that can never be broken. Parents and children who have buried loved ones together share valuable perspectives on life. And *true* friends will find ways of showing their faithfulness... of proving that you and your loved ones are not to be forgotten.

For over a year, one of our friends sent us cards every month... little messages of love on Father's Day, Mother's Day, the boys' birthdays, and the anniversary of the boys' deaths. Other friends will call from time to time to say, "I just wanted you to know that I was thinking about the boys this week." It's a ministry of small... but tremendously appreciated... messages.

Disaster intensifies what is already there. Relationships can be strengthened. True friends can demonstrate their faithfulness. Feeling like you are going to die can teach you a lot about the way you want to live.

When There Are No Words

13

WORK CAN SAVE YOUR LIFE

At some point, people will begin to expect you to return to what they perceive to be a *normal* life. Actually, your life will never be normal again. You will learn to be pleasant, productive, and functional but things will never be the same again because an integral part of what used to be *you* has been torn away. But... even in the earliest stages of feeling around for your land legs... the familiar moves and thought patterns of work can have remarkable therapeutic value.

Whatever was your *life's work* before your loved one died can become *the work that can save your life* in the early weeks and months of grief. Again, *you* are the only one who knows the right timing for your return to work. You shouldn't make the mistake of going straight from the funeral to the office — the guilt for that ploy will catch up with you later. But neither should you take an indefinite leave of absence on the assumption that you will never be able to function again.

My experience has been that getting back into familiar work patterns is very hard to bring yourself to... but tremendously helpful once you do it. The worst part... the part that makes you want to put if off forever... is the dread of crossing the emotional threshold with your former work associates.

They are dreading it as much as you are. They are scared to death that the first word they speak to you will cause you to shatter into a million pieces. Some will want to bring you pillows and stir your coffee. Others will actually treat you with a rough and gruff all-business attitude as if to say, "Nothing has happened. We're all business around here and we expect you to snap out of this grief thing, jump back in, and pull your share of the load."

Perhaps the most baffling human reaction of all is the inclination to pretend that nothing has happened. If you came back to work with your leg in a cast and your arm in a sling, everybody in the place would want your personal account of how it all happened. But... when you walk in short-of-breath and absent-of-mind because death has stolen a part of your self... people will talk about everything except your obvious loss. And this phenomenon occurs... strangely enough... at the time in your life when you most need to talk about that stolen loved one.

I found it quite amazing to see how instantly the atmosphere changed as soon as I took the initiative and inserted Tim or Don into the conversation. That was easy enough to do since both our boys were adept at putting the things they said in humorous and quotable form. Before and after they died, the boys' quotes have been some of my best contributions to conversations and business meetings.

It is an amazing transition to watch. Everyone around you is whispering and walking softly. Then... in the context of the normal discussion... you make some casual reference to your lost loved one or something they once said. For an instant, everyone freezes. They watch anxiously to see if you will scream and melt away like the witch in the *Wizard of Oz*. When you don't... the room warms up, everyone lets out a sigh of relief, and a *real* conversation begins.

I have learned from this experience (and from years of working around people with disabilities) that one of the most insensitive and dishonest things we do to each other is to ignore the obvious. If a person is in a wheelchair, it is ridiculous for us to talk with them day after day without the wheelchair ever entering the conversation. If a person is a member of *any* minority or has any obvious uniqueness... and we pretend that we just haven't noticed... the relationship is founded on a lie because we have mutually agreed that our communication will be less than 100 percent honest.

Obviously, I am not encouraging anybody to intentionally embarrass another person or pry into subjects that are painful. But... time after time since the boys died... I have had fascinating encounters and turned strangers into friends by establishing early in the conversation that I *do* see the obvious. As I sat in the sauna at the health club one day, a man entered whose left arm hung limply at his side. Instead of mumbling a hello and sitting quietly, I simply asked, "How did you lose the use of that arm?"

His response was instant, honest, and opened up a fascinating life story of the accident that had permanently damaged the arm and a lifetime of over-compensation that had caused him to give up a job he hated in corporate management and become... of all things... a sculptor and maker of fine furniture. Before the boys died, I would have never asked the question that opened up that man's interesting life to me. But now... having been the one with the obvious problem that people were intentionally ignoring... I am the first to ask about the obvious.

I try to ask gently, sincerely, and fully prepared for a rejection of my expressed interest. So far, I am yet to experience that rejection. On the contrary, I have met fascinating people who are grateful for a chance to bypass the small talk and honestly discuss things that really matter. I learned a lot from Tim and Don while they lived and... now that they have gone... they continue to teach me things about life.

The work that saves your life does not always have to be work that you were involved in before the tragedy. Kay took up a new hobby after the boys died and it has filled her time, focused her energy, and yielded valuable new perspectives. Shortly after the boys' deaths, Kay came across some genealogical information on some ancestors she had never known about. The information led her into a time-consuming exploration of her ancestors and their family history. She had always loved puzzles and genealogy proved to be the ultimate one-piece-at-a-time involvement.

She awakes in the mornings with something she needs to accomplish: a visit to the archives, a new microfilm to read, or records to abstract. Her research has blended with our vacation time to take us to five or six states and one foreign country. She bought some advanced computer software for genealogical record-keeping and now helps people in our area who are new to that kind of software.

Kay and I have had some enjoyable trips in search of old burial plots that were long ago surrendered to the vines and undergrowth. We have slogged through the mud, raked back the leaves, squinted to make out ancient inscriptions. You might assume that the last thing any couple needs when they have recently buried two of their three sons would be to go searching through the rural countryside for lost family graveyards. And yet, the opposite has been true.

Kay's hobby has given us a new and valuable perspective on the death of loved ones. Every burial plot speaks eloquently to the fact that death is as natural as life and that it has only been in our generation that the deaths of children became unusual. We found the graves of Kay's great grandparents in rural Arkansas. We had known that they raised eight children. But... until we read the inscription on their large tombstone... we had not known that they had *six* other children who died in childhood. It was a new and valuable perspective for us. It did not make us miss Tim and Don any less but it did put the shortness of their lives into the enlightening perspective of history. I am told that... even today, in third-world countries... parents often refrain from naming a baby until it has survived through its first year of life.

Perhaps our world could benefit from more frequent visits to its cemeteries. I am always impressed as I walk through historic cemeteries at the effort made by stone cutters to assure that names and dates will never be forgotten. They chisel the letters deeply and clearly but eventually the weather and the passage of time win out. You walk by those inscriptions and maybe you can recognize one word or one date. The rest of the wording has joined the oldest parade of all: from life to death... from known to unknown.

If you are an atheist, I recommend visiting graveyards often... to keep perspective on the brevity of life and the inevitability of death. If you believe in life after death, I recommend visiting graveyards often... to keep perspective on the brevity of life and the wonderful fact that life never ends — it just passes into another realm. Who would have thought that cemeteries would have good things to say to people in grief? For us, they have.

One final note about work (or hobbies) and their ability to save your life as you wade through your grief. As has been true in almost every chapter of this book, *you are the one* who knows when and how much work is good for you. People around you will make every effort to keep you busy. They will volunteer you for things. They will invite you to all kinds of activities. They have good intentions. They assume that... if you are busy... you are not thinking about your loss. Nothing could be farther from the truth. You can be as lonely in a crowd as in a desert. Even when your hands are *building*... your heart can be breaking.

Only you can discern the fine line between pushing yourself too much and pushing yourself too little. Sometimes it helps to mentally compare a *physical* injury to the *emotional* one you are fighting. If you had a broken leg instead of a broken heart, you would give it time to heal. You would not let friends talk you into walking on it before you were ready. You would obey *your* feelings... knowing *whose* leg was in question. So, treat your heart with the same common sense you would show your leg.

Recognize what your friends *intend* instead of what they are *saying*... and tell them no... unless you really want to go along. Be sensitive to your own energy levels and plan your own pace of return to activity. Letting others keep your body busy will not control your mind... and it will exhaust your body. Work can save your life if you find the work that *distracts* from your grief... instead of *adding* to it.

14

GET OUT OF TOWN

I don't have a lot to say about this piece of advice. The title says it all. Particularly when the holidays are approaching... or when your loved one's birthday is on the horizon... or when the anniversary of a death date is about to occur... get out of town. It is advice you will hear often and it is good advice. You don't have to spend a lot of money or escape to the South of France... but get out of town.

At a support group one night, I listened to parents who had lost children as they discussed the gathering gloom of the approaching Thanksgiving and Christmas holidays. One father summed it up for the whole group when he said, "I think it would be great if we could just skip from November first to February first." Everyone in the group agreed.

Holidays are *family* times and... when part of the family has been ripped away... the holidays can only emphasize the loss. Kay and I have found time after time that changing the scenery and the routine during the last half of

December has helped to dull the pain. Travel doesn't *remove* the pain but it does help to *dull* it.

A few people have told me that being at home with family all around is a most therapeutic way for them to spend holidays. They wouldn't think of leaving home and missing out on those soothing family times. It's just one more proof that we each have to find the formula that works for us. Whatever works for you, go with it.

Kay and I tried once staying at home through the holidays. Once was enough. We intend to be out of town on December 15th from now on. Our income fluctuates from year to year so we can't always plan expensive getaways. But there are inexpensive ways to change the scenery and the routine. For us, any change helps.

15

FIRST YOU LOSE THE CAT...
THEN YOU LOSE THE KITTEN

Before the boys died, I never had a clue about the intricate and multiple ways that you lose a loved one. I thought... along with everybody else... that your loved one dies, you grieve, you get over it, and life resumes. Now, I know it's not that simple.

I have found myself describing the never-ending process of loss with the words... *First you lose the cat... then you lose the kitten*. To understand what I mean, you have to know about my idea that nature pulls a very clever trick on us when it starts out cats as cuddly little kittens... dogs as cute little puppies... and teenagers as lovable little babies. If the order were reversed... and they started out in their troublesome stages... there would be a lot fewer pet owners and parents.

On the morning that the policeman stood in our cold den and told us that the boys had died, there was one thought that flew through my mind that I am reluctant even now to admit. I thought, "Well, I won't have to worry about them any longer. I won't have to worry about whether Tim will go back to college. I won't have to worry about Don's safety in the mountains of Honduras."

There was relief. Part of the burden of raising teenagers had been lifted from my shoulders. The relief was short-lived. The burdens and guilt of the grief process soon took over and I even felt ashamed for having thought of relief. It was an honest feeling — those two cats were... at that point in their lives... providing me with a lot more stresses than satisfactions.

First you lose the cat. And... if that cat has gone through a long illness that pushed you to the edge of your physical and emotional endurance... it's natural to feel a little relief when it ends. If you could just lose the cats... if you could just watch their unrelenting pain finally stop... it would be a lot easier to let them go.

The problem is... losing those kittens. You start going through the mountain of stuff they had saved. You come across the creations in paper and yarn and clay that one of those cats made when he was a kindergarten kitty. You hold those little creations in your hands... and you have to lose the kitten all over again.

Kay tells me that one of the hardest things for her in the first year after the boys died was going to the super market. Think about it. What do you do in a super market? You walk up and down aisles and you make decisions. You say to yourself, "Tim likes that. Don likes that. I could get this for dinner... except that Tim doesn't like it."

Every super market decision has a family memory connected to it. You'd never expect a package of spaghetti or a can of creamed corn to leave you crying in the aisle at the store. Songs on the radio... kids at the mall... smells in a bakery. The world is filled with reminders... reminders that hurt.

You pass a framed snapshot on the wall that has been hanging there for years and you are immediately transported back to the time the kids made their own costumes for Halloween. You look at the snapshot and you are transported back to that Halloween. And you have to lose those little kittens all over again.

There's the cast that Tim wore from his wrist to his shoulder the time he broke his little arm. That cast looks so tiny now... nothing like the grown-up arm on the boy who died. You hold that miniature cast in your hand... and you lose that cute little kitten all over again.

I had forgotten the way I used to tease Don when he was a curly-headed kid of six or eight. If he complained about one of my rules, I would say, "You'll see, Don. One of these days, you'll be the daddy and Don Jr. will think you are being too strict."

Don would wrinkle has freckled nose and smile. We joked about Don Jr. a lot. Every now and then, it hits me that I will never see Don Jr. There won't be weddings for Tim or Don... or career victories... or family milestones. First you lose the cat. Then... forever and ever... you keep losing the kitten.

Every Valentine they made for you... every poem they wrote in school... every certificate of achievement... every drawing they made... is another cute and cuddly kitten you have to surrender. You lose different parts of them at different stages of your grief. You lose them over and over again. Perhaps the optimistic would say that you are blessed with memories to last you for many years. The less optimistic would probably say... *First you lose the cat... then for the rest of your life... you're going to be losing the kitten.*

16

GETTING MAD AT GOD

The accidental or untimely death of a loved one is an experience that will let you know what you really believe about God and the degree of his intervention in life. You can talk confidently about your faith for years but... when life suddenly drops a sand bag on you... and God doesn't step in to keep it from hitting you... you are about to find out which one of the many forms of God you really believe in.

Kay was mad at God for a long time after our boys died. Fortunately, she was honest and secure enough to be able to describe her status in those exact words and our friends were able to let her speak her mind without penalty. As time has passed, Kay has articulated for both of us the fact that she was living under an assumption that many people hold: that... as long as we are trying to be God's people and serve him... he will protect us and not let anything happen to us.

It's a naive approach but one that is quite understandable for those of us who have grown up hearing stories about Old Testament characters. The concept was always presented as such a simple formula. When the children of Israel obeyed God, things went along well for them. They had peace and contentment and the land flowed with milk and honey. But... when they stopped obeying God... everything fell apart, there was famine, and the bad guys from the neighboring countries came in and punished everybody.

If that's the God we were worshipping, it is quite reasonable to be mad at him. We were trying to do our part and God slipped up and let this terrible thing happen. Of course... if you had asked us years ago if that was the concept we held about God... we would probably have said no. The truth is that most of us never really scrutinize our concept of God until it suddenly appears to let us down.

Rabbi Kushner wrote a book that attempted to speak to this dilemma of where God was when we counted on him to protect us. *When Bad Things Happen to Good People* is a popular book and it probably has helped a lot of people. It hasn't worked for me. I have tried to read it several times but I can't ever get very far into it. I keep getting hung up on the premise that is expressed in the book's title.

We humans are very quick to pronounce ourselves "good people" and to assume that things that happen that we don't like are "bad things." Except in the natural self-centeredness of grief, neither one of those assumptions are justified. If bad things were happening only to bad people, you can bet a lot more people would start being good. And... with enough passage of time... a lot of things that seem disastrous turn out to be blessings. And vice-versa.

In spite of the fact that I believe in God... in his concern for me... and in the fact that he hears and answers prayers... I never felt like the boys' deaths proved anything one way or another about God. Why do I think our boys died? They broke the law of carbon monoxide. They were sitting in a car that had a bad muffler. If you break the law of carbon monoxide... you're going to die. If you step off a cliff and break the law of gravity... you're going to die.

Our tendency to flippantly and automatically categorize things as "bad" simply because they are unpleasant for us is not a very mature way of looking at life. Somebody dies and we say "That's bad." It's not necessarily so. They were eventually going to die anyway. We should more accurately say, "They died... and that makes me unhappy." Or simply that, "I am shocked... and I miss them tremendously due to the suddenness of their departure."

Given time... and the perspective of God... the boys' deaths may not be a *bad* thing at all. Since we do not have their *continued* lives to compare with their *ended* lives, we really cannot accurately judge the badness or goodness of their departure. I do know this: for several years I had regularly prayed to God that he would "deliver my boys from the temptations of this world." I used those exact words. In retrospect, I have to wonder whether my prayer was answered when my boys were quite literally removed from the temptations of this world.

I believe God was watching that night as the boys died. I picture them rising from their dead bodies and moving into an eternal realm and... as Rick so eloquently expressed it in some of his own writing... "I am confident of our reunion."

17

TIME DOESN'T HEAL
ALL WOUNDS

Kay and Rick and I continue in what we now know to be a never-ending process of coping. We are functional... but there are some wounds that time can never heal. As a boy, I always assumed that there would come a day when I would wake up and discover that I had become a man. It didn't happen that way. The boy is still inside fighting with the man on a daily basis. And, as grieving parents, we may have assumed that there would come a day after several years when we would be *over* the deaths of Tim and Don and Bryan. Not so. The pain continues. It doesn't come as often now... but when it does... it hurts as much as it did that very first morning.

Most of the insights that I have gained from this experience... the things that I wish somebody could have told me on the day of the funeral... have been learned with the passage of time. Contrary to popular wisdom, time does *not* heal all wounds. Some people *die* from wounds. Others just learn to live with scars. I used to jokingly say that "you can get used to measles if you have them long enough."

That was back when I thought that time healed all wounds and that you could get used to anything. Now, I know there are some hurts that never stop hurting... no matter how faded the scars may be.

There are people all around you who have lost loved ones in sudden and tragic ways. They will tell you about it if you ask them. But... unless you bring it up... you will not likely hear their stories. They are functional again. They even smile. But they are never going to be the same again as they were before death reached in.

I heard a person say recently that the intensity of the grief you are feeling only goes to show the intensity of the love you felt for the person or persons you lost. I like the sound of that because it underscores the value of admitting all your feelings of grief... really giving it all a chance to come out and be heard. But... on the other hand... that saying worries me a bit. It makes me feel a little guilty as my pain occurs less frequently. It makes me wonder, "If I'm not crying every day, does it mean my love was not real and genuine... or that it is disappearing?"

And that brings me full circle to the most important thing I learned from the whole experience... and... have to continue re-learning from time to time. *The way I grieve... is the way that is right for me.* The minute I start trying to monitor and adjust my ways of missing Tim and Don and Bryan... trying to conform my grief to others' descriptions... or even to what I think others might think appropriate... I am adding unnecessary extra baggage to a process that is tough enough already.

In the first week or so after the boys died, I happened to be visiting an office where I had worked before. I was talking with Nancy. I knew that Nancy's grandmother had died fairly recently and she and I were comparing notes about the characteristics of grief: the inability to focus your concentration on things you need to think about... the inability to think about anything else but the person you've lost... even the inability to take a deep breath of air. My question for Nancy was, "When does it ease?"

I don't remember Nancy's exact words but the gist of her answer was, "The awareness never completely goes away but I can say that... somewhere around the one year mark... I began to notice that I was feeling much more normal again."

For me... Nancy's promise of one year became a tangible, realistic point on a calendar I could understand. It proved to be true for me as well. There was no magic switch that clicked on the one-year anniversary but... somewhere around a year... things began to feel more normal again.

Kay and I attended some classes and read some books about grief. In an effort to simplify an irresistibly complex topic... the leaders almost always described the five stages of grief... or the seven stages of grief... or however many a particular author or speaker had identified. The problem is that our emotions refuse to be governed by checklists. And... while the authors and speakers always added that these steps did not happen in the given sequence... it always seemed to me to be implied that... if you had just been in the shock stage... you could expect to move into the denial stage next... and after that... whatever came next.

My experience, however, has been that I was more likely to have all the stages at one time in one inseparable mass... then go for a period when none of them were bothering me... only to be hit by the whole gang later on. I can honestly say that... even years after the boys' deaths... the fact can suddenly hit me with all the power it carried on that first pre-dawn December 15th. I experience the *full force* of the emotional hurricane over and over again... but with longer periods of quiet in between.

Time doesn't heal all wounds. It just puts more space between the times you remember the events that gave you those wounds.

18

MY PRAYER FOR YOU IS...

that you will have peace.

that you will have good grief.

that you will be honest with yourself... letting out what is within you... and refusing to govern your ways of grieving by what you think others might be expecting that you ought to do.

that you will allow your loved ones the same right to their own ways of grieving... never assuming that they should want to cry when you feel like crying... or talk when you feel like talking... or sit and stare when you want to.

that both your life and your death will be greatly enhanced by the perspectives that enter your life when a loved one exits your life.

that you will become daily more comfortable with the realization that... as Don often told me... "Death is just a part of living."

ACKNOWLEDGMENTS

I'd like to acknowledge first and foremost *you*, the reader. The book really was written for and because of people like you... people in pain. My first thought when the boys died was that one unique tribute a professional writer could give the boys would be not to tell their story... not to turn their deaths into another writing assignment. It was several years before I realized that some of the things we had learned in our grief were actually soothing and helpful to wounded people I shared them with in conversation. I began to think those ideas might belong in a form that could spread them even farther.

The list of people who have enabled the writing of *When There Are No Words* is long and filled with many who would prefer not to be singled out. Some of that number have already been somewhat obscured by the intentional use of first names *only* in the retelling of our story.

Continuing the intimacy of first name thank you's... let me mention some specific groups and the ways they have helped. When the book was only a first draft, some wonderful friends took the time to read and provide valuable feedback and suggestions. It became a much better book through the loving touches of Rob and Karen, Bob and Carole, Bud and Carole, Jerry and Peggy, Carl and Donna, Tim and Barbara, Jack and Rosemary, Dan and Barbara, and A.P.

Once the book was a manuscript in search of an understanding publisher, there were some who read and encouraged and others who encouraged without even reading. They include Jerry of the AT, Bill and Peggy of UMCom, Tyra of WinShape, Larry of Rutledge Hill, Bob and Myron of J&J, the Grief Class of Decatur, the Compassionate Friends of Atlanta, Lawrence of Charles Press, and Eugene Wheeler, Publisher of Pathfinder Publishing.

And the last word in acknowledgments is "Kay"... the blue-eyed love of my life who really meant it when she signed on "for better or worse" and "Rick"... our brown-eyed first-born who continues to impress us with his creativity and make us proud with his maturity."

Charlie Walton
October 1995

RESOURCES

Organizations

National Victim Organizations

Each of the following provide information and referral services to assist victims in locating their nearest local program.

American Association of Suicidology
4201 Connecticut Ave., N.W. Suite 310
Washington, DC 20008
(202) 237-2280

Mothers Against Drunk Driving (MADD)
511 E. John Carpenter Fwy. #700
Irving, TX 75062
(214) 744-6233
Victim Hotline 1-800-GET-MADD

NOVA (National Organization for Victim Assistance)
1757 Park Rd. N.W.
Washington, D.C. 20010
(202) 332-6682

National Victim Center
2111 Wilson Blvd., Suite 300
Arlington, VA 22201
(703) 276-2880

National Headquarters Of Support Organizations
Parents of Murdered Children
100 E. 8th Street, B-41
Cincinnati, OH 45202
(513) 721-5683

The Compassionate Friends
P. O. Box 3696
Oakbrook, IL 60522-3696
(708) 990-0010

National Medical Resources
American Trauma Society
8903 Presidential Pkway. #512
Upper Marlboro, MD 20772-2656
1-800-556-7890

National Head Injury Foundation
1776 Massachusetts Ave., N.W.
Washington, D.C. 20036
(202) 296-6443

Sunny Von Bulow Coma & Head Trauma Foundation
555 Masison Ave. #32001
New York, NY 10022
212-753-5003

Spinal Cord Society
Rt. 5, Box 22A, Wendell Rd.
Fergus Falls, MN 56537
(218) 739-5252

National Funeral/Burial Resources
National Funeral Directors Association
11121 W. Oklahoma Ave.
Milwaukee, WI 53227
414-541-2500,
(FISCAP - arbitrates consumer
complaints)

For Those Who Have Lost An Infant Or Child
AAID
P.O. Box 20852
Milwaukee, WI 53220

A.M.E.N.D.
Aiding Mothers and Fathers Experiencing Neo-Natal Death
Maureen Connelly
4324 Berrywick Terrace
St. Louis, MO 63128

Centering Corporation
1531 N. Saddlecreek Rd.
Omaha, NE 68104
(402) 553-1200
Information on those who have lost an infant or suffered miscarriage

Compassionate Friends
P.O. Box 3696
Oak Brook, IL 60522

Empty Arms
6416 Wyndham Ct.
Erie, PA 16505

National Foundation for Sudden Infant Death
330 North Charles St.
Baltimore, MD 21201

Parents of Murdered Children
100 East 8th St. Suite B41
Cincinnati, OH 45202

S.H.A.R.E.
Source of Help in Airing and Resolving Experiences
St. John's Hospital
800 E. Carpenter
Springfield, IL 62769

For Widowed Persons
AARP Widowed Persons Service
601 E. St., N.W.
Washington, DC 20049
(202) 434-2277

Jewish Widows and Widowers
Beth El Temple Center
2 Concord Avenue
Belmont, MA 02178

Parents Without Partners
7910 Woodmont Avenue
Washington, DC 20014
(202) 638-1320

Theos
They Help Each Other Spiritually
The Penn Hills Office Building
11609 Frankstown Rd. Room 306
Pittsburgh, PA 15235

Suicide
American Association of Suicidology
4201 Connecticut Ave., N.W. Suite 310
Washington, DC 20008
(202) 237-2280

Survivors of Suicide
Sharry Schaefer
3251 N. 78th St.
Milwaukee, WI 53222

Suicide Prevention Center, Inc.
184 Salem Avenue
Dayton, OH 45406

Youth Suicide National Center
1825 I. Street NW Suite 400
Washington, DC 20006

General Grief
Accord Inc.
P.O. Box 5208
Louisville, KY 40205

A.M.E.N.D.
4324 Berrywick Terrace
St. Louis, MO 63128

Hand
P.O. Box 62
San Anselmo, CA 94960

Hoping
Sparrow Hospital
1215 E. Michigan Ave.
Lansing, MI 48909

The Life Clinic
1026 S. Robertson Blvd.
Los Angeles, CA 90035

Prevention Center, Inc.
184 Salem Avenue
Dayton, OH 45406

Unite
Jeane's Hospital
7600 Central Avenue
Philadelphia, PA 19111

Other Helpful Organizations
American Cancer Society
19 W. 56th St.
New York, New York
(212) 586-8700

Continental Assn. of Funeral & Memorial Societies
33 University Square, Suite 333
Madison, WI 53715
(800) 458-5563

Elizabeth Kubler Ross Center
So. Route 616
Head Waters, VA 2442

Foundation of Thanatology
630 W. 168th St.
New York, NY 10032
(212) 928-2055

Loving Outreach for Survivors of Sudden Death
P.O. Box 7303
Stn. M. Edmonton, Alberta
Canada T5E 6C8

Remove Intoxicated Drivers
RID
P.O. Box 520
Schenectady, NY 12301

National Hospice Organization
1901 North Fort Meyer Drive, Suite 402
Arlington, VA 22209

READING RESOURCES FOR ADULTS

Augsburger, David. *Caring Enough to Forgive/Not to Forgive,* Regal Books, 2300 Knoll Drive, Ventura, CA 93003.

Bard, Morton, and Sangrey, Dawn. *The Crime Victim's book,* Brunner/Mazel, Psychological Stress Series, 19 Union Square, New York, NY 10003.

Bolton, Iris. *My Son My Son,* Bolton Press, Atlanta, Georgia.

Carlson, Lisa. *Caring for Your Own Dead,* Upper Access Publishers, One Upper Access Road, P. O. Box 457, Hinesburg, VT. 05461.

Cato, Sid. *Healing Life's Great Hurts,* Chicago Review Press, 213 W. Institute Place, Chicago, IL 60610.

Donnelly, Katherine F. *Recovering From the Loss of a Child,* Macmillan Publishing Co., 866 3rd Ave., New York, NY 10022.

Donnelly, Katherine F. *Recovering From the Loss of a Sibling.* Dodd, Mead & Company, 71 Fifth Avenue, New York, NY 10003.

Grollman, Earl A. *Living When a Loved One has Died,* Beacon Press/Fitzhenry & Whiteside Ltd., Toronto, Canada.

Grollman, Earl A. *What Helped Me When My Loved One Died.* Beacon Press, 25 Beacon Street, Boston, Massachusetts 02108.

Grollman, Earl A. *Talking About Death: A Dialogue Between Parent and Child,* Beacon Press, 25 Beacon Street, Boston, Massachusetts, 02108.

Knapp, Ronald J. *Beyond Endurance:When a Child Dies,* Schocken Books, 62 Cooper square, New York, NY 10003.

Kubler-Ross, Elisabeth. *On Children and Death,* Macmillan Publishing Company, 866 Third Avenue, New York, NY 10022.

LaTour, Kathy. *For Those Who Live,* P.O. Box 141182, Dallas, Texas 75214, (for surviving siblings).

Lord, Janice Harris. *Beyond Sympathy,* Pathfinder Publishing, 458 Dorothy Ave., Ventura, CA 93003.

Lord, Janice Harris, *No Time For Goodbyes,* Pathfinder Publishing, 458 Dorothy Ave., Ventura, CA 93003.

Manning, Doug. *What to Do When You Lose a Loved One,* Harper & Row, 151 Union St., San Francisco, CA 94111-1299.

Neiderbach, Dr. Shelly. *Invisible Wounds:* Crime Victims Speak, Haworth Press, 28 E. 22nd Street, New York, NY 10010.

Osterweis, Marian et al Eds. *Bereavement: Reactions, Consequences and Care,* National Academy Press, 2101 Constitution Avenue NW, Washington, D.C. 20418.

Rando, Therese A. *Parental Loss of a Child,* Research Press, 2612 N. Mattis, Champaign, IL 61821.

Rando, Therese A. *Grieving: How to Go on Living When Someone You Love Dies,* Lexington Books, 125 Spring St., Lexington, MA 02173.

Saldona, Theresa. *Beyond Survivial, Bantam Books, 666 Fifth Ave., New York, NY 10103.*

Schiff, Harriet S. *The Bereaved Parent,* Penguin Books, 40 W. 23rd Street, New York, NY 10010.

Schiff, Harriett S. *Living Through Mourning,* Viking-Penguin, 40 W. 23rd St., New York, NY 10010.

Westberg, Granger E. *Good Grief,* Fortress Press, Philadelphia, PA.

Staudacher, Carol. *Beyond Grief: A Guide for Recovering from the Death of a Loved One,* New Harbinger Publications, 2200 Adeline St., Suite 305, Oakland, CA 94607.

Stearns, Ann K. *Living Through Personal Crisis,* Thomas More Press, 223 W. Erie Street, Chicago, IL 61610.

Tengbom, Mildred. *Help for Bereaved Parents,* Concordia Publishing House, 3558 S. Jefferson Ave., St. Louis, MO 63118.

When Hello Means Goodbye (when infants die before, during or shortly after birth) Perinatal Loss, 2116 NE 18th Avenue, Portland, OR 97212.

Wolterstorff, Nicholas. *Lament For a Son,* William B. Eerdmans Publishing Company, 255 Jefferson Avenue SE, Grand Rapids, Michigan 49503.

INDEX

ORDER FORM

Pathfinder Publishing of California
458 Dorothy Ave.
Ventura, CA 93003-1723
Telephone (805) 642-9278   FAX (805) 650-3656

Please send me the following books from Pathfinder Publishing:

_____Copies of **Beyond Sympathy** @ $11.95 $____
_____Copies of **Injury** @ $12.95 $____
_____Copies of **Living Creatively**
      With Chronic Illness @ $11.95 $____
_____Copies of **Managing Your Health Care** @ $9.95 $____
_____Copies of **No Time For Goodbyes** @ $11.95 $____
_____Copies of **Quest For Respect** @ $9.95 $____
_____Copies of **Sexual Challenges** @ $11.95 $____
_____Copies of **Stop Justice Abuse** @ $7.95 $____
_____Copies of **Surviving an Auto Accident** @ $12.95 $____
_____Copies of **Violence in our Schools, Hospitals and**
      Public Places   @ $22.95 Hard Cover $____
      @ $14.95 Soft Cover $____
_____Copies of **Violence in the Workplace** @ $22.95 Hard $____
      Violence in the Workplace @ $14.95 Soft $____
_____Copies of **When There Are No Words** @ $9.95 $____
           Sub-Total $____
      Californians: Please add 7.25% tax. $____
      Shipping* $____
           Grand Total $____

I understand that I may return the book for a full refund if not satisfied.

Name:_____

Address:_____
_____ZIP:_____

*SHIPPING CHARGES U.S.
Books: Enclose $2.75 for the first book and .50c for each additional book. UPS: Truck; $4.25 for first item, .75c for each additional. UPS 2nd Day Air: $10.75 for first item, $1.00 for each additional item. Master and Visa Credit Cards orders are acceptable.

About The Author

Charlie Walton is a full-time wordmonger... providing scriptwriting, copywriting, and speechwriting services to business and educational clients. Doing business as *The Wordmonger,* Charlie has developed a diverse customer clientele among telecommunication, education, training, church, and marketing executives.

Charlie is a ghostwriter for other people's books and speechwriter for many corporate executives. *When There Are No Words* is his first nationally published book under his own name.